THE ART
OF
NEGOTIATING

Gerard I. Nierenberg

A FIRESIDE BOOK
Published by Simon & Schuster, Inc.
NEW YORK

To Donald A. Nierenberg

First Fireside Edition, 1986

Published by Simon & Schuster, Inc.
Simon & Schuster Building
Rockefeller Center
1230 Avenue of the Americas
New York, New York 10020

Published by arrangement with E.P. Dutton, Inc.

FIRESIDE and colophon are registered trademarks of Simon & Schuster, Inc.

Manufactured in the United States of America

10 9 8 7 6 5 4 3 2

Library of Congress Cataloging in Publication Data

ISBN: 0-671-62999-9

INTRODUCTION

When THE ART OF NEGOTIATING® was first published in 1968, it introduced a new discipline and a new era. For the first time, the word "negotiating" acquired respectability. No longer was it synonymous with horse trading and other adversary relations. Instead, it might be seen as a process that could profoundly affect every type of human relationship and produce lasting benefits for all participants. Furthermore, as a discipline, all of the techniques that bring a negotiation to a successful conclusion can be learned and put into practice by everyone from the novice to the most experienced negotiator.

This book is known worldwide and in its first thirteen years, it has been translated into ten languages besides English. It has become recognized as a universal system that can be applied to some of the most vexing problems of the human existence—relations between people, businesses and governments. Why, indeed, "do the heathen rage so furiously together, and the people imagine a vain thing?" One reason surely is that they have real or imagined unmet needs. This is a given part of the human condition.

The unique quality of THE ART OF NEGOTIATING® is that it does not deal with these needs by ignoring, repressing, or trying and failing to solve them. Instead it offers a system, easily understood by people throughout the world, that can meet those needs. Even more important, it can meet them in ways that are satisfying and beneficial to both sides: the heathen and the true believers, the people and their government.

A major problem with the trial and error method of learning to negotiate is that you have to endure many errors before you accidentally stumble on a reasonably satisfactory solution. It is like the man who made a habit of kissing strange women: invariably, he was slapped in the face, but he consoled himself with the memory of the nice kisses he had received in the past. THE ART OF NEGOTIATING®, with its proven methods of changing relationships for the benefit of both parties, helps you avoid the slaps in the face and permits both parties to enjoy the kisses.

This book is based on scientific principles. That is, it considers observable, even commonplace, "facts" of human behavior and organizes them into a structure that can be duplicated again and again. Of course, no two negotiations are ever exactly alike. However, once you are familiar with the pattern of successful negotiation, as explained in this book, you will never regress to the haphazard methods you have used in the past.

THE ART OF NEGOTIATING® might aptly be compared to the laser—a device for the creation, amplification and transmission of an intense beam of *coherent* light. This is not a book of esoterica. Every detail in it has probably been accepted by you as given a long time ago. The book's value (and purpose) is to take these random "facts" and details and shape them into a coherent stream of enlightenment. Instead of being weighed down with unsolvable problems, you will find your life enriched by your ready access to methods that have been used successfully by hundreds of thousands of people who have read this book and attended THE ART OF NEGOTIATING® seminars. You will find that by using them, all of your negotiating experiences are easier to handle, more enjoyable and infinitely more profitable than ever before.

Gerard I. Nierenberg

CONTENTS

> "LET US BEGIN ANEW, REMEMBERING ON BOTH SIDES THAT CIVILITY IS NOT A SIGN OF WEAKNESS, THAT SINCERITY IS ALWAYS SUBJECT TO PROOF. LET US NEVER NEGOTIATE OUT OF FEAR. BUT LET US NEVER FEAR TO NEGOTIATE."
>
> —JOHN F. KENNEDY

I

ON NEGOTIATING

Recently two of my sons were squabbling over some leftover apple pie, each insisting that he should have the larger slice. Neither would agree to an even split. So I suggested that one boy cut the pie any way he liked, and the other boy could choose the piece he wanted. This sounded fair to both of them, and they accepted it. Each felt that he had gotten a square deal.

This was an example of "perfect" negotiation.

A salesman is trying to close a large sale. Basically his proposition is acceptable to the prospective customer—but there are still a number of questions to be answered. How much discount can he give? Who will have to warehouse the bulk of the order—buyer or seller? Can delivery be sped up? Will the seller agree to give the buyer price protection on reorders for two years?

Buyer and seller *negotiate* the sale.

In a time when the computer has made many jobs obsolete, the role of negotiator grows in importance. For we are all negotiators.

WHAT IS NEGOTIATION?

Nothing could be simpler in definition or broader in scope than negotiation. Every desire that demands satisfaction—and every need to be met—is at least potentially an occasion for people to initiate the negotiating process. Whenever people exchange ideas with the intention of changing relationships, whenever they confer for agreement, they are negotiating.

Negotiation depends on communication. It occurs between individuals acting either for themselves or as representatives of organized groups. Therefore negotiation can be considered an element of human behavior. Aspects of it have been dealt with by both the traditional and the new behavioral sciences, from history, jurisprudence, economics, sociology, and psychology to cybernetics, general semantics, game and decision-making theory, and general systems.

Yet the full scope of negotiation is too broad to be confined to one or even a group of the existing behavioral sciences.

Every day, the *New York Times* reports hundreds of negotiations. At the United Nations and in capitals around the world attempts are made to settle the "small" wars. Government agencies negotiate with the United States Congress for appropriations. A utility company confers with a regulatory agency on rates. A strike is settled. Two companies agree to merge but must obtain the consent of the Justice Department. A small but valuable piece of real estate changes hands. These are the types of negotiations that the *Times* might describe any day of the week. Occasionally there may be a spectacular agreement, such as the nuclear test ban treaty, to attract worldwide attention. But even more important, at least to the people that participated in them, are the countless negotiations that are not mentioned in the *Times* or in any other newspaper.

Even that age-old negotiating situation, subject matrimony, is but slightly influenced by the vaunted computer. The computer may take over the role of matchmaker—but it is merely predicting that two particular negotiators have the best chance of reaching a satisfactory agreement.

Up to the present time, no general theories were available to guide an individual in his day-to-day negotiating activities. All too frequently we have had to learn to negotiate the same way we learned such things as sex—by trial and error. The man who claimed to have thirty years' experience in negotiation might simply be making the same mistakes every year for thirty years.

Thus most of our knowledge about negotiation, unfortunately, has had to come from our limited personal experience. And most people impose further restrictions on the negotiation process. Here, for example, is an excerpt from a study by the Committee for the Judiciary of the U.S. Senate released a few years ago:

> To an American, negotiation is the least troublesome method of settling disputes. Negotiation may be exploratory and serve to formulate viewpoints and delineate areas of agreement or contention. Or it may aim at working out practical arrangements. The success of negotiation depends upon whether (a) the issue is negotiable (that is, you can sell your car but not your child); (b) the negotiators interested not only in taking but also in giving are able to exchange value for value, and are willing to compromise; or (c) negotiating parties trust each other to some extent—if they didn't, a plethora of safety provisions would render the "agreement" unworkable.

The Commitee's three requirements for successful negotiation drastically limit the area of possible action. Children are sold, even in America, as the occasional revelation of a black-market baby ring clearly indicates. And a parent whose child is kidnapped would not hesitate to negotiate for its release. All issues must be considered negotiable whenever there are human needs to be met.

As for the second requirement, it is impossible to foresee in any negotiation what the outcome is going to be. Therefore it is impossible to anticipate in advance that either party will be "willing to compromise." Compromise is usually arrived at during the normal course of bargaining. It develops naturally as a result of a thorough examination of the facts and the opposing and also the common interests of the negotiators involved. Although compromises may be worked out as a result of a negotiation, the parties should not enter into discussions with the sole intent of compromising. Even in a "simple" negotiation, a number of issues are involved. It would scarcely be to anyone's advantage to compromise on each of them. The old saying, "The wheels of diplomacy often turn on the grease of ambiguity," is applicable here.

It is better to enter into a negotiation without self-imposed limitations, ready to seize any advantage that is offered.

The Commitee's third stipulation is almost impossible to meet. Generally, the parties involved in a negotiation do not "trust" each other. Indeed, the handling of other people's mistrust is the skilled negotiator's stock in trade. To summarize, I doubt whether there would be negotiations if the Committee's three conditions were the prerequisites to success.

A Real-Life Example

Negotiation isn't always neat. And it is often not nice.

Commuters who park their cars at railroad stations have become aware in recent years that there are moves afoot that imperil their "rights" to park. They might be interested in an example of the kind of behind-the-scenes negotiation that can curtail those "rights."

Some time ago, the real estate department of a railroad approached a real estate firm. The problem: the railroad needed money. Was there some way they could utilize their vast excess property to make money?

The real estate firm was interested. But there were certain facts that had to be faced. The first fact was a legal one—you cannot obtain clear title to railroad property. The railroads have not purchased their land outright. They have received much of their land either by condemnation or by a deed in lieu of condemnation. Both of these methods vest a reversionary right in the former owner, the right to recover land if it is not used for railroad purposes.

After much digging and considerable thought, the real estate firm's legal advisors (my law office) came up with a solution. This involved, not purchasing the land, but rather renting it for ninety-nine years.

And here is where the second fact began to crop up—the "human" factor. People who work for large organizations are not often inclined to stick their necks out. The railroad attorneys would take some convincing.

A title company was approached and finally persuaded to state that the plan was legal. The title company was even willing to back up the statement with a title insurance policy. When issuance of the policy was actually committed, the railroad attorneys had no alternative but to agree that the procedure was valid.

The next step involved getting the land released from the railroad mortgage. The law firm studied railroad mortgages in general, and this case in particular. A useful point emerged. Most of the railroads placed their mortgages in the 1930's and 1940's. After World War II, people lost confidence in the financial condition of the railroads, and there was little demand for railroad bonds or mortgages. These mortgages did not contain a clause that covered property acquired later.

The solution? Make a bookkeeping transaction. Take some land that the railroad had acquired *after* the mortgage—and exchange it with the mortgage trustee for the land covered by the mortgage.

This idea brought another party into the picture. The mortgage was controlled by a trustee. The real estate people approached the trustee with this appeal: anything that improves the financial condition of the railroad benefits all concerned. Furthermore, the trustee was shown the statements by the title company and the railroad lawyers asserting that the thing could be done. After some discussion, the trustee agreed to the land switch.

Now came a new phase of the negotiation. A railroad station was chosen. The excess property surrounding it was earmarked for development. Plans were submitted to the town for the construction of a shopping center.

The result was electrifying. The townspeople had been parking on this land for many years. They assumed that it was their *right* to do so. The prosperity of many of the town's businesses depended on the happiness and continued residence of the very people who parked on that land.

The town zoning board had never even bothered to zone the railroad property. Now, reacting adversely to the pressure from the citizens, they put the land in the category known as "Business B," one foot of parking for every foot of business space. This was not arbitrary, since the surrounding land was similarly zoned. But the citizens continued to apply pressure and within a week the land was rezoned "Business A," which required two feet of parking space for every one foot of business space. This was the first time that such a regulation had ever been applied in the town.

The real estate company might have had pretty good grounds on which to fight the regulation. Instead they went to the railroad, obtained more space along the right of way, and complied with the stricter zoning.

Having no further "out," the town granted a building permit. Permit in hand, the real estate firm approached a food chain, and a lease was negotiated and signed. The lease called for the chain's Florida architect to submit plans for the interior of the store within one month.

Meanwhile a full-scale political hurricane had blown up in the town. The "out" party made a major issue of the situation. The "in" party, seeing its mandate slipping away, arbitrarily revoked the permit. There was nothing for the real estate company to do but go to court. There was little question that they could win the case, if it were heard without bias.

In most negotiations of any importance there is an element of luck. Although the judges of the state Supreme Court in this county were predominantly Republican, one lone Democrat had gotten elected on a fluke. With luck (and a little maneuvering) the case came up before this lone Democrat—who was less hampered by party requirements and much more likely to provide an immediate and unbiased hearing.

The town, having elected all Republican officials, realized this too. The town attorney approached the real estate men and asked, "Can't this be disposed of?" "Certainly!" was the answer. "Grant us the building permit." Because of the political climate, the town representative explained, this couldn't be done. Instead, the town —knowing fully the title restrictions and so on—would like to try to buy the property.

For a price, all real estate is for sale. Furthermore, money was tight at the time, and the real estate people were having a little trouble with financing. The town offered attractive terms and the deal was consummated.

End of negotiation? No. The lease with the food chain was fairly explicit in stating that, if municipal regulations prevented the building of the shopping area, then the lease was canceled. The chain was told that as soon as another convenient location could be found, their store would be built. But this promise was not enough for the food chain. They instituted a suit for breach of contract.

This kind of suit was the last thing the real estate company needed. They asked the chain, "Can't you see that this was not within our control?" The answer: "Well, we are a public corporation, and we owe a certain duty to our stockholders."

The real estate lawyers thought this one over. Yes, a public corporation has a duty to its stockholders. It also has the responsibility of reporting to the stockholders every major suit that is filed against them.

Could it be that the chain would find a suit embarrassing? Well, the real estate men thought, let's find out.

The original lease had called for submission of architects' plans within a month. The plans had arrived late. At the time no one had considered this a factor in the proceedings, but, technically, the chain was in default. So—claiming that proper submission of the plans might possibly have enabled building to start and avoided all the delay—the real estate firm instituted a large suit for damages.

Upon service of the summons, the food chain contacted the real estate organization. "Will you drop your suit? If so, we will drop ours." The answer was, "We like our lawsuit, and have no intention of dropping it." It was a stalemate. Neither side proceeded with its suit. This was the situation for about six months.

Then my law firm received an urgent phone call from their counterparts on the food chain side. Could they come over immediately? My firm answered, "We're tied up. We'll call you back."

Intuitively we felt something had changed. Intense research was instituted. We found that the chain was negotiating with a larger public corporation that wanted to take them over. Obviously the hanging lawsuit was an obstacle.

The chain people were called. The meeting was to take place at the offices of the real estate lawyers. Terms were dictated. The chain agreed to pay $25,000 in cash. Both parties were to drop their lawsuits.

This complex negotiation—or series of negotiations—contains good and bad examples of the elements that go into successful negotiation, the elements that this book will cover.

The Basic Ingredients

Human beings in this case reacted on one another in all their fascinating and contradictory splendor. A *knowledge of human behavior* is essential to any negotiator.

The negotiators who *prepared*—who did their homework—were

ahead of the game.

All parties to the negotiations made certain *assumptions*. Some of these assumptions held up, some did not. Successful negotiation can depend upon your own assumptions—and your anticipation of the other side's.

Techniques of negotiation—*strategy* and *tactics*—came into play. For example, the *reverse* strategy of the counter lawsuit is a technique we will discuss at greater length.

Each of the parties had *needs*, direct and indirect, which they wanted to satisfy. When the approach took into account the other side's needs, it was successful. When needs were ignored—when the negotiation was played as a game, with a total winner and a total loser—both sides came a cropper.

The anticipation and satisfaction of needs is central to the method that we are discussing. Let's look at a different kind of negotiation in which *needs* were all-important.

Party A to this negotiation was a broad-ranging investor and speculator, one of the "money men" who have achieved prominence in today's business climate. Let's call him Johnson.

Johnson has acquired a number of varied enterprises—hotels, laboratories, automobile laundries, movie theaters. For a number of good reasons he decided that he wanted entrée into the magazine publishing field.

A "finder" put Johnson in touch with a magazine publisher whom we shall call Robinson. For some years Robinson had been publishing and editing a good magazine in a specialized but growing field. The magazine had never actually "taken off"—but since Robinson did most of the work himself, costs were low and Robinson made a comfortable living. Robinson was good, probably the best in his particular area of publishing. Large publishers had made offers to acquire him and his magazine, but for one reason or another nothing had ever come of them.

Johnson decided that he wanted the magazine. More to the point, he wanted the services of Robinson, whom he saw as the nucleus of an expanding chain of specialized magazines. After a couple of luncheon get-togethers, the understanding was that they would get down to serious negotiation.

Through his own observation, and through investigation, Johnson had found out some things about Robinson. Robinson, with justification, held his own ability in extremely high regard. He had little use for the larger publishing houses—"factories," as he called them.

Furthermore, Robinson now had a wife and a growing family. The high-risk joys of being an independent operator were beginning to pall on him. The late hours in the office—particularly those spent on noncreative tasks like bookkeeping—were no longer congenial.

And Robinson mistrusted "outsiders"—those who were not part of his creative world. He particularly mistrusted "business types," especially those in the noncreative end of publishing.

When the time for negotiation came, Johnson opened by confessing his complete ignorance of magazine publishing. To him, one of the greatest values in their association would be that he would have a professional who would call all the shots.

Then Johnson placed on the table a check for $25,000. "Naturally we are talking about a lot more money," he said, "in stock and long-range benefits. But I feel, in any agreement like the one I hope to make with you, there should be immediate and tangible benefit."

Johnson introduced Robinson to a number of his associates, particularly his business manager, who would be at Robinson's disposal and who would relieve Robinson of any onerous chores that he wanted to get rid of.

As they proceeded to talk, Robinson held out for an immediate "clean" deal—cash—not stock in the parent company, which had strings attached. But Johnson emphasized long-term security, and showed how the parent stock had grown in value over the past few years and how a stock interest would tie them together. He further underscored his need for Robinson's full creative energies, undiminished by conflicts about another job, retirement, or whatever.

In the final analysis, Robinson turned over his magazine, and his own services, for a contracted period of five years. There was a $40,000 payment in cash. The rest was in stock, which could not be sold for five years.

Robinson came away with his major needs fulfilled. He would have help with the more "distasteful" parts of the business, while remaining assured of complete control in the creative area; he had backing for expansion; he had financial security; and his conflicts were resolved.

And Johnson had acquired a valuable property and the services of a uniquely valuable man for less than he might have been willing to pay.

What made this a successful negotiation? Knowledge of human nature, preparation, strategy—all combining to *satisfy needs*.

SALES NEGOTIATIONS

Today many businesses have begun to recognize the broad scope and importance of effective negotiating techniques. Some progressive sales organizations attempt to provide their salesmen with these techniques along with selling kits. The business of selling franchises, for example, has been very successful along these lines.

Almost every conceivable product and service is sold through franchise distributors. Prices for these franchises can run from hundreds to hundreds of thousands of dollars. Although the prospective franchise purchasers usually have had sufficient business experience to raise the funds necessary to go into the venture, they are rarely skilled negotiators. And their preconceptions about negotiating techniques often keep them from obtaining all the concessions they could get.

As an illustration, the prospective franchise purchaser shows up at the sales office, usually in response to a newspaper ad that had set forth the merits and potentials of the particular franchise. He walks in with a chip-on-the-shoulder attitude: "OK, show me." The seller has been carefully trained in handling this type of person. Rather than oppose the purchaser's belligerent attitude, he redirects it and adopts a program called "qualifying the purchaser." He starts with a simple series of questions asking the purchaser his name, address, previous experience, and references, leading the potential purchaser into a position where he, the purchaser, feels he must show the franchise salesman that he is capable of handling the franchise and will be a valuable addition to their organization. Instead of being "sold," the purchaser has been negotiated into *selling himself*.

In another situation, a franchiser was selling a complex franchise. An involved sales presentation was necessary in order for it to be clearly understood and absorbed. The franchiser found that buyers—who were seemingly convinced as they left the office—subsequently lost interest.

It turned out that the difficulty arose when the buyer could not clearly explain the proposal to his wife, lawyer, or accountant. They raised troublesome doubts that could have been resolved only by a careful explanation of the proposal. Faced with the dilemma of going into a business he could not explain, the potential buyer lost his initial interest and enthusiasm.

The franchiser felt that the solution to this problem was neither to keep the buyer from discussing the proposal with whom he chose, nor to direct a salesman to present the same·deal several times to satisfy all the doubters. Instead an attempt was made to guide the buyer to informed sources who thoroughly understood the proposal, and thus could answer his *need to know and understand*.

Thereafter, whenever the sales presentation was made, a great emphasis was placed on the point that the franchise was unique, and only a few people were capable of fully understanding it or giving any advice about it. The buyer, however, still needed to satisfy himself by outside verification. This need was answered by ending the presentation with the statement, "If you wish to purchase this franchise, you must do the following: first check it out with the Better Business Bureau; then speak to at least two actual owners of franchises on this list. After you have done that, call us for another meeting." No attempt was made to contact the prospect until he had invested the time and interest to check with these sources. It appears that when his *need to know and understand* is satisfied in this way, the buyer is fully convinced, and the final closing follows without complications.

LABOR-MANAGEMENT NEGOTIATIONS

Collective bargaining has evolved as a tool for settling of labor-management disputes. Recognizing this technique as a sub-division of negotiation, both sides have initiated courses and studies in labor negotiation. As a result, highly trained negotiators have dominated both sides of the bargaining table.

In the words of Professor Leon M. Labes, "Few who have had first-hand experience in the field of labor-management relations will deny that decisions reached by collective bargaining are the only ones that are completely satisfactory. Everything that can be done to encourage and foster such negotiations must be done, and many new techniques have properly been developed." In the United States these industrial negotiations are carried on under at least two ominous threats, one from each side of the bargaining table: labor's power to strike, and management's power to close, relocate, or lock out. All labor-management negotiators are constantly aware that in the event of their failure to achieve a settlement, one or both of these threats will be implemented.

In spite of the tremendous strides labor has made as a result of collective bargaining, it has generally been content with its limited goals. One who might attempt to improve the situation is rewarded with dismissal. This is what happened to David J. McDonald in 1965, when he failed to win reelection as president of the United Steel Workers of America. He had attempted to bring about settlement of minor incidents and disputes before they became points of disagreement.

McDonald worked closely with his brilliant general counsel, Arthur J. Goldberg, to put an end to the long and costly strikes that had plagued the industry since World War II. Their cooperation resulted in the establishment of a human relations committee.

The committee, composed of four top representatives of the industry and of the union, met throughout the year to discuss problems and make mutually beneficial suggestions, all of this without the necessity of working under contract deadlines. This would appear to be an ideal method, one that would lead to ideal solutions. In fact it worked so well that the steel industry began to be pointed to as a model of what could be accomplished with industrial relations.

Then something went wrong. McDonald lost the union presidency to I. W. Abel, who campaigned under the slogan "Give the union back to the membership." In devising a better collective bargaining system, McDonald, Goldberg's student, had neglected one essential aspect of negotiating, namely *communication*. He failed to keep the membership closely acquainted with exactly what was happening. Complete secrecy was permitted for the new human relations committee, in order to allow its members freedom to discuss problems without fear of the industry and membership reaction. Although the end was desirable, the means permitted an insurgent group taking advantage of McDonald's failure to inform and communicate with the membership.

The intellectual leadership of unions and management today utilize negotiation only to a limited degree. That limitation is termed collective bargaining. The larger scope of negotiation includes aspects of communication; it considers the effects upon a total community and also recognizes collective bargaining as an instrument for protecting the general public welfare. It is apparent that these and other higher considerations have been neglected to date.

The future will undoubtedly bring some type of change in the rules and climate of industrial collective bargaining. Strikes against the public interest will probably be forbidden or eliminated through some form of government participation.

How will such a change affect the techniques of negotiation? The answer is, not at all. The concepts of how to negotiate are more basic in character and rise above the particular set of rules or regulations of collective bargaining that happen to be in vogue at any particular time.

REAL ESTATE NEGOTIATION

In the following negotiation, see if you can spot the elements of human behavior, preparation, assumptions, strategy and tactics, and need fulfillment.

A plain postcard is not usually the most interesting item in a stack of mail. However, a real estate associate and I discovered an exception one morning when we were reviewing offers of properties submitted by brokers. On a postal card was a broker's offer to sell an $800,000 property. If the broker had meant to attract our attention, he certainly succeeded. We had to know more about the property.

When we investigated, my associate Fred and I discovered a most interesting situation. The property was controlled by a trust company, and under ordinary circumstances the land itself would probably have been worth $800,000. But these were no ordinary circumstances. A fire had virtually destroyed the building on the property, leaving only a shell that was in danger of collapsing. The building department had already served the trust company officers with a summons demanding immediate action to make the property safe. Instead of the staid day-to-day routine of adminstering the property, the trust company was confronted with an unfamiliar and threatening situation, one it seemed unable to cope with. The only solution the officers could come up with was to sell immediately. Fred and I decided to relieve them of their dilemma, but of course on our terms.

We submitted our offer: $550,000 if they would take back part of the purchase price in a twenty-year mortgage, or, as an alternate proposal, $475,000 in cash. The property manager at the trust company refused even to entertain our written offer. Fred then called him and requested an appointment, which was reluctantly granted.

Fred came to the point at once. He told the property manager that the board of directors would have to make the ultimate decision whether to sell or not, that the manager was only their agent. Therefore, if the manager refused to act, Fred would bypass him and submit the offer to the board himself. This threat—to his *security*—worked. Our offer was submitted to the board.

The board, being concerned with the dangerous condition of the property, had limited themselves to a single strategy: to accept the first firm offer they received. Our cash offer was accepted. Quite naturally the property manager was extremely unhappy when he notified us by phone. He said the contract would be ready at five o'clock Friday and I had better be there at five o'clock sharp. When Fred and I arrived, we were presented with a carefully worded thirty-page document.

The manager, still unhappy, scowled. "Here is the contract. Don't dot an 'i' or cross a 't.' Take it or leave it just as it is." After reading it, we decided to take it. Thirty minutes after arrival, we left the manager's office. We were now the contract owners of the property. Only the formality of the title closing remained before we became full legal owners.

As so often happens in negotiations, a "mere formality" became the springboard for still further discussion and adjustment of the agreement. Incredibly, a few hours after we signed the contract, a second fire swept the building, completely demolishing the damaged structure. The next morning I hurried to my office and spent the weekend deep in legal research. By Monday morning I had completed my "homework." Fred and I waited in my office for a phone call from the trust company. The telephone rang promptly at nine o'clock. We arranged a meeting that morning at the offices of a prominent Wall Street law firm.

The senior partner of the law firm was very cordial as he ushered us into his private office suite, and opened the discussion: "We are not here to discuss law, but merely to get rid of a very difficult situation." I nodded in agreement. He went on to explain what we already knew, that the streets around the property were closed because of the dangerous condition, and that the trust company was more anxious than ever to be rid of the property. The company and its lawyers insisted we take over the property immediately and eliminate the hazard.

I countered with the statement that Fred and I had not had a chance to discuss the matter thoroughly and that we would need a little time. A large conference room was put at our disposal, but before he left us alone the attorney took me aside. "Remember," he said, "in this contract your client waived all the statutory protection." The statute he referred to would have placed the fire loss on the seller. By waiving it, the loss would be ours.

"You're absolutely correct," I said carefully. "We waived all our statutory rights. But," I added, giving him the benefit of my weekend of research, "that means we have only the right that existed under common law before the statute was passed." The common law generally had placed a fire loss before title closing on the purchaser, but the courts had made many exceptions to this rule of law. I reminded the attorney of an exception applicable to our situation. In the event something specific, such as a building, was sold with the land, and the building was damaged by fire, the loss would be the seller's. The seller must deliver exactly what he contracts to sell or there must be an adjustment in price.

"Now," I continued, "that wonderful contract that you drew up made it extremely clear what we were purchasing. It made it so clear that not once but four times it stated we were buying a *partially* damaged building. Now it is completely demolished. We are entitled to a partially damaged building or an adjustment in price."

In the conference room, Fred and I put ourselves in the trust company's position. If the matter went into litigation, it would take at least two years to determine the equities involved. During that time the trust company would have to pay $25,000 a year in taxes on the property and would lose an equal amount in interest to be earned on our purchase price. According to our conservative estimate, the company would lose at least $100,000 even if it won the case.

We went back with our proposal: we would take over the property immediately instead of two or three weeks later if they reduced the purchase price by $100,000. A stunned silence was followed by an outburst from the property manager. But in a few minutes we agreed to a reduction of $50,000 and immediate possession of the property. Thereupon Fred and I became "fee title absolute owners" of a valuable piece of land and, of course, a *completely* demolished building—requiring far less expenditure for clearing the land.

The negotiation described above dealt with a fairly complex situation. Yet even to a person with no experience in real estate transactions, most of its elements are recognizable. This is because underlying every action and counter-reaction was a desire to satisfy a basic human need. The *satisfaction of needs* is the goal common to all negotiations, and therefore it can provide us with a structural approach to the study of the negotiating process. This book will review the elements of the behavioral sciences applicable to the process, then define and develop the Need Theory of Negotiation, and finally present a variety of illustrations of the Need Theory in action. An understanding of this structure will permit you to operate in a negotiating situation with new power and depth of understanding. Negotiation will become the art of expanding possibilities.

II

THE COOPERATIVE PROCESS

In a successful negotiation *everybody wins.*

NOT A GAME

Negotiating has often been compared to a game. A game has definite rules and a known set of values. Each player is limited in the moves he can make, the things he can and cannot do. True, some games have a greater element of chance than others, but in every game a set of rules governs the behavior of the players and enumerates their gains and losses. In games the rules show the risks and rewards. However, rules of this sort are not available in the unbounded life process of negotiation. In negotiating, *any* risks that are known have been learned from broad experience, not from a rule book. In a life situation the negotiator ordinarily has little or no control over the complex variables, the innumerable strategies, that the opposer may bring into the struggle. Even

more difficult is to know the value structure upon which the opposer bases his strategy.

To look upon negotiation as a game to be played is to enter
into the bargaining in a purely competitive spirit. With this attitude, the negotiator strives against other individuals for a goal
which *he alone* hopes to attain. Even if he could persuade an opposer to "play" such a negotiating game, he would run the risk of
being the absolute loser rather than the winner. In post–World
War II Japan, some businessmen required that their employees
study military strategy and tactics as a guide to successful business
operations. How many of these employers realized that comparing
business with war was only a metaphor? How many saw that the
goal of a successful business deal is *not* a dead competitor?

The objective should be to achieve *agreement*, not total victory.
Both parties must feel that they have gained something. Even if
one side had had to give up a great deal, the overall picture is one
of gain.

Newspapers Folded

Negotiation, then, is *not* a game—and it is not war. Its goal is
not a dead competitor. A negotiator ignores this point at his own
peril.

A classic example is the recent history of the newspaper business
in New York City. Bertram Powers, head of the printers' union,
became nationally known as a man who "drives a hard bargain."
With the aid of a couple of paralyzing strikes, the printers in New
York achieved what seemed to be remarkable contracts. Not only
did they obtain higher wages, but the newspapers were forbidden
to institute such money-saving practices as the automated setting
of market tables.

The printers won their points at the negotiating table—because
they held out to the end. But the newspapers were forced into an
economic straitjacket. Three major newspapers merged and finally,
after another long strike, folded, leaving New York with one evening and two morning papers—and leaving thousands of newspaper people with no place to work. The negotiation was "successful," but the patient died.

"Cooperative Egotism"

Think of negotiation as a *cooperative enterprise*. If both parties enter the situation on a cooperative basis, there is a strong likelihood that they will be persuaded to strive for goals that can be shared equally. This does not mean that every goal will be of the same value to the participants. But it does mean that there is greater possibility for each participant to reach successful cooperative goals.

However, the competitive attitude need not be abandoned. It serves as an integrating process, a rivalry that coordinates the activities of individuals. A single side of a scissors by itself cannot cut. Competition that permits each man to measure his competence or means against the other's—and to be rewarded proportionally—is really a cooperative achievement.

A great impetus to reaching an accord is the search for common interest levels. Franklin D. Roosevelt stated: "It has always seemed to me that the best symbol of common sense was a bridge." However, let us add what Robert Benchley says: "It seems to me that the most difficult part of building a bridge would be the start."

Always be on the alert to convert divergent interests into channels of common desires. In exploring these channels, both parties to the negotiation may be stimulated by the idea of sharing common goals. These goals are reached by finding mutual interests and needs, by emphasizing the matters that can be agreed upon, and by not dwelling on points of difference. Queen Elizabeth II, during her tour of West Germany in 1965, urged this course of action when she said: "For fifty years we heard too much about the things which divided us. Let us now make a great effort to remember the things which unite us. With these links we can begin to forge a new and better understanding in the future."

What has been called the French definition of love, "cooperative egotism," can be applied to this approach to negotiation. An example occurred when I represented a trade association of radio and television servicemen in New York. At one meeting the order of business included seeking better ways of attracting members, and doing more for the existing members. The entire problem was reduced into one word, publicity. The question was how to get publicity.

It seemed perfectly logical to seek publicity on radio. After all, the servicemen were the radio stations' distant cousins. But thinking along these lines, the trade association presented an offer to each station. In return for free publicity on the air, the servicemen would advertise the name of the radio station, place program material in his store window, and—even more important to the radio station—make sure that the station was properly received on every set that he repaired. In addition, the repairman would make a survey of the entire area that he covered and report to the radio station any problem areas in which their transmission was not properly received. The first contract closed for this reciprocal arrangement amounted to $40,000 worth of free radio publicity for the servicemen's association.

There are many advantages to the cooperative approach. Results can be greater and the solution more lasting. Children are taught that one plus one is two and two minus one is one. Throughout their lives most people are inclined to apply arithmetical principles in their judgment of what is desirable or undesirable. It is not difficult, then, to understand the person who applies the "I win, you lose" (plus/minus) arithmetical concept to his negotiations. He is merely using simple equations in his judgment of human behavior.

However, these equations do not apply to *all* human efforts. Cooperative human efforts can be cumulative when ideas, rather than material goods, are exchanged. If you and I exchange ideas, where each of us had one idea we now each have two, and thus one plus one equals four. Certainly no one has lost by this transaction. It is possible that in making other people wealthier, happier, and more secure you will have more of your own needs satisfied. This is, in fact, an ideal result of any negotiation.

Many negotiations conducted in a highly competitive manner have ended in what seemed to be a complete victory for one side. The alleged winner was in possession of everything he wanted and the loser had suffered a humiliating defeat. However, such a "settlement" will rarely stay settled. Unless the terms arrived at have been advantageous in some way to the "loser," he will soon seek means of changing the settlement. Unlike a game, there is no "end" to a life negotiation situation. Many times clients of mine are convinced that they have scored a complete victory over their opponents and have forced the losing side to accept absolute defeat. I attempt to explain that there are numerous continuing elements and side effects that may well affect the "final" consummation of the deal.

Even if my client has been able to overcome all objections from his opponent's attorney and accountant, the one-sided, forced settlement is not final, it will not stick. Often a wife, as final adviser, will upset the prior agreements. Husbands do have a habit of discussing their business affairs with their wives, and a wife will not hesitate to point out that he has agreed to a bad deal and that no preliminary agreement is sacred. In other cases, after quiet reconsideration, the dissatisfied party—or even a third party—may begin a lawsuit to set aside or reorganize the unfavorable settlement. An overwhelmingly one-sided settlement breeds trouble and in the end will only prove to be a great waste of time and effort. It contains the seed of its own destruction. Yet rigidly competitively oriented people often wonder why they can never seem to conclude anything. They say they work hard, but luck or life never seems to break for them. Something always goes wrong.

This should not be surprising. We could complete few tasks without the complete cooperation and assisting efforts of others. Who would drive an automobile if he could not rely on other people to comply with traffic regulations?

There are other advantages to the cooperative approach. Results can be greater, solutions more lasting.

A few years back a well-known professional athlete wanted more money in his yearly contract. For several seasons he had attempted to do his own negotiating but had failed to achieve what he considered a satisfactory settlement. Although the athlete was a man of considerable wealth and intelligence, he was shy and, by his own confession, no match for his hard-driving general manager. Furthermore, the general manager had an ace up his sleeve—the "reserve clause" that makes it impossible for an athlete to move from one team to another.

The manager invariably forced the ball player to sign for less than he deserved. The athlete had become so demoralized that he conducted negotiations with this man solely by letter. He felt defeated before he even started to negotiate.

Then an agent approached the athlete. He suggested a solution. True, the "reserve clause" precluded any threat of playing for another team. However, there was nothing to keep the player from dropping out of sports.

Despite the athlete's shyness, he had a pleasant personality and was not bad looking. People with far less in the way of presence have made it in show business. Negotiations were begun with an independent film producer. There was talk of a five-year contract.

Now, suddenly, the pressure was on the general manager. The fans would react adversely if the star left the team, and business would drop off. The athlete negotiated an enormous increase. The next season other members of the team used the same techniques. They pitilessly "held up" the manager for as much as the traffic would bear.

Had the manager been satisfied to negotiate, rather than dominate, he would have directed his efforts toward the cooperative goal of improving the club rather than toward resisting just demands. The lesson to be learned is, never press for the "best" deal and thereby corner your opponent. As Edna St. Vincent Millay observed, "Even the lowly rat in adversity has courage to turn and fight."

REACHING A LIFE BALANCE

Few negotiations proceed smoothly. I have participated in literally thousands of negotiations, and no two are ever alike. Sometimes a client managed to secure close to 100 per cent of the pie —when he was bargaining from a position of strength. At other times I have been forced to negotiate with almost all the strength massed on the opposite side of the table. In such a case one has to be content with salvaging as much as possible from the situation.

In instances where I have been able to get my client only a small piece of the pie, I try to console him, and myself, with the story of Baron Z. Donnson. The Baron, a White Russian, had established himself in Rio de Janeiro. I met him several years ago at a party given in honor of his eightieth birthday. His new bride was a beautiful Brazilian in her early twenties. All the men at the party were gathered around this charming creature, monopolizing her attention throughout the evening. I sat with the Baron, chatting and drinking, and as the evening wore on we grew quite friendly. I finally mustered the courage to ask him why he had married such a young girl. He put his arm around my shoulder and replied quite simply that at his age it is better to have 10 per cent of a good thing than 100 per cent of nothing.

Negotiating is give and take. However, each side is watching the opposer for any clue to his prejudices that may provide a negotiating advantage.

Plutarch's metaphor is apt. He said, "As bees extract honey from thyme, the strongest and driest of herbs, so sensible men often get advantage and profit from the most awkward circumstances. We should learn how to do that and practice it, like the man who flung a stone at his dog but missed it and hit his stepmother, whereupon he exclaimed, 'Well, not so bad, after all.' "

It is fascinating to observe two master negotiators battling it out. As a rule they are able to arrive at a settlement very quickly. They go directly to the heart of the problem and waste no time on extraneous matters. Each side, after an initial period of probing and feeling out the other, promptly realizes that he is dealing with a master and that a quick solution is forthcoming. Many labor strikes could actually be settled at a first or second meeting but for political or economic reasons, the agreement is not verbalized until a later date.

However, when the bargaining is conducted with all the coolness of professional gamblers at a poker game, this is merely a surface mannerism. In actuality, experts do not play a negotiating game. They are adept at the art of compromise and accommodation. They are fully aware of the necessity for finding a common ground of interest, and they avoid the pitfalls of a competitive I-must-win-the-game attitude. At the earliest possible moment in the negotiation, each side manages to convey to the other its maximum concessions and the minimum concessions expected in return. This is not done explicitly, but subtly, by innuendo and deliberate tip-offs. Such skills and techniques, arrived at through long experience and training, enable the master negotiators to reach a satisfactory settlement. Examples of this type of negotiation are seen daily in the United Nations. However, remember that the final decisions are not within the control of these professionals. They act as agents for their individual governments and cannot effect satisfactory settlements to world problems by themselves.

WHEN CONTROLS BECOME UNCONTROLLABLE

Sometimes, when an opponent seems "on the run," there is a temptation to push him as hard as possible. But that one extra push may be the one that breaks the camel's back.

Simply stated, one of the first lessons the negotiator must learn is *when to stop*. Negotiation, like alcohol, does not conform to the simple mathematical principles we learned as children. It's that little extra "one for the road" that can kill you. There is a *critical point* in negotiation beyond which the reaction—like that of an atomic pile—can become uncontrolled and destructive. An example may be found in the extensive research that was conducted into the causes of unscheduled work stoppages—strikes, accidents, unavailability of supplies—occurring a few years ago in the coal mines around Manchester, England. It was found that when the group size in the individual work force *exceeded a critical number*, the stoppages occurred.

So the negotiator's aim should never be "just one more." He must sense when he is approaching the critical point—and stop short of it. *All parties to a negotiation should come out with some needs satisfied.*

This can't happen when one of the parties is demolished.

It's all too easy to lose sight of this principle. In the heat of negotiation, one can be carried away.

Once I was retained by a client who was the last tenant in an office building scheduled to be demolished. The new owner planned a skyscraper in place of this four-story building. All the other tenants had moved out. My function, in addition to protecting my client's rights, was to work out a solution acceptable to both parties.

The landlord recognized that, to get my client out of the building, he would have to pay money. His question was, "How little?" The landlord first approached me personally. (In my opinion, this was a mistake. Later we will take up the value, in certain situations, of bargaining through an agent who has only limited authority.)

"How much do you want?" the landlord asked. "I'm sorry," I replied. "You are the one who is buying. I am not selling." This placed the burden of opening the negotiations upon him. So far so good. We both recognized that my client was in a very strong position. He had two years to go on his lease, and the landlord needed to get started immediately.

The opening offer indicated the landlord's willingness to pay moving expenses and the differential in rent. I declined to get into anything other than the cash figure he was offering—"How much?" After some byplay he offered $25,000. I refused even to consider it. He left the office.

The landlord's next tactic was delay. But this worked against him, because my client was perfectly willing to stay put. When delay did not work, the next approach came through the landlord's attorney. I told the attorney that when he came up with a figure that was in the "ball park," we would negotiate. "Fifty thousand," he said. "Not in the ball park," I replied.

Approaches continued, with the offer getting higher. I never named a figure until the final stages. But I did do some homework, figuring out what the landlord had paid for the building, what it would cost him to keep the building vacant, what it would cost him to hold the mortgage commitments until the end of my client's lease.

I came up with a figure of a quarter of a million dollars. Knowing that this was speculation, and not wanting to squeeze the last dollar, I cut this in half. The landlord's lawyer was forced to bid against his own figure and finally settle for $125,000. It seemed to me that this was a solution that satisfied everyone.

However, I was in for a surprise. When the landlord's lawyers delivered the check, a young attorney said to me, "Five dollars more and you might have had a crane hit the building." The crane was on the property, and it just might have struck the old building—"accidentally"—so that it would be declared a hazard that had to be torn down. In that case my client might have gotten nothing.

Now a few things may be noted about this. It was not the most intelligent thing in the world for the opposing lawyer to say. However, I realized that he meant what he said. (When a negotiation is over and the opponent is upset, his tendency is sometimes in the other direction—to make you feel bad by indicating that there was a lot more to be had if you had just held out for it.)

My client was vulnerable. If I had realized how close I was to the top figure, I would have settled at a lower price. The danger of going too far is not worth the risk.

Master negotiators are of course a rare commodity. Negotiation in itself is a useful tool of human behavior and as such can be mastered with study and practice. But to show how short we all fall of the "ideal," here is a quotation from *How Nations Negotiate*, by Fred Charles Ikle: "The compleat negotiator, according to seventeenth- and eighteenth-century manuals on diplomacy, should have a quick mind but unlimited patience, know how to dissemble without being a liar, inspire trust without trusting others, be modest but assertive, charm others without succumbing to their charm, and possess plenty of money and a beautiful wife while remaining indifferent to all temptation of riches and women."

Successful negotiations are not sensational. No strikes, law suits, or wars occur. Both parties feel that they have gained *something*. Even if one side has to give up a great deal, the overall picture is one of mutual gain.

To sum up thus far: negotiation is a cooperative enterprise; common interests must be sought; negotiation is a behavioral process, not a game; in a good negotiation, *everybody wins something*.

These are planks that make up the platform from which we will view some of the pleasures and complexities of successful negotiation.

III

PEOPLE

The cooperative approach to negotiation—the approach which postulates that all parties must come away having gained *something*—is based on a simple but important premise.

Negotiation takes place between human beings.

You cannot negotiate with a computer.

Therefore, to negotiate successfully, you must have a knowledge of people. Alexander Pope said, "The proper study of mankind is man." For the negotiator, the study of man is not only proper; it is essential.

The ways of learning about man are as diverse as man himself. We learn by reading, by listening, by observing, by finding out how people react—and have reacted—in certain situations. Every newspaper story, every casual conversation, every train or plane ride gives you a chance to build up your armory of information about human behavior.

In this chapter we consider and suggest some of the ways to find out all you can about the behavior of people—and how you can make that knowledge work for you in the negotiating situation.

INSTINCTIVE? RATIONAL?

According to Machiavelli, "Wise men say, and not without reason, that whoever wishes to foresee the future must consult the past; for human events ever resemble those of preceding times. This arises from the fact that they are produced by men who have been, and ever will be, animated by the same passions, and thus they must necessarily have the same results."

Negotiations involve the exchange of ideas between human beings directed toward changing a relationship. Gathered at the conference table will be a heterogeneous group of individuals with the most varied personalities, characters, and emotions. Viewed superficially, human behavior sometimes appears to be disorganized, haphazard, chaotic. The newspapers tend to confirm this impression. Senseless crimes, acts of aggression, often sparked by absurd trivialities, and eccentric conduct of all kinds account for many news items every day. With such evidence, it is hard to think of man as a reasonable being, and harder still to believe that his behavior follows a rational pattern.

How should we study behavior? What sort of tests or experiments should we perform? What should be the nature of our approach? The answers to questions of this kind have undergone radical changes during the last fifty years. The various approaches can be classified as functional psychology, structural psychology, associationism, behaviorism, Gestalt psychology, psychoanalysis, hormic psychology, holistic psychology, phenomenology, existentialistic psychology, humanistic psychology, transactional psycology, biosocial psychology. In the first decade of this century, psychology was dominated by the behaviorist school under the leadership of John B. Watson. The behaviorists were inspired by the brilliant results in animal psychology achieved by Morgan and Thorndike. Man, Watson declared, should be studied like any other animal. Behavior should be observed like the phenomena of all other natural sciences, such as chemistry, physics, physiology, or biology. No behaviorist, Watson argued, has observed anything that he can call consciousness, sensation, perception, imagery, or will. Therefore all such terms should be dropped from descriptions of man's activity. Experiments should be confined to objective observations of the results of stimulus and response. A simple example of the type of experimentation pursued by the behaviorist school is the careful investigation of the act of eye blinking when the cornea is touched. Thousands of experiments of this kind were performed and a mass of useful data was accumulated.

The behaviorist school's approach, however, was subjected to critical attacks by the rising tide of the dynamic psychologists. They said man was not a mere machine. He cannot be explained purely in terms of stimulus and response. The how and why of behavior, a man's mental life, his emotions, cannot be banished from science. In Germany, the Gestalt psychologists revolutionized our ideas on how we perceive things and how we solve problems. The psychoanalytic school of Freud, Adler, Jung, and others developed theories of mental stresses and strains, of the influence of the unconscious, that have exerted a great influence on modern thought. The behaviorists of today do not limit their studies to trivial muscle twitches, but, with a modified definition of "behavior," they occupy a most useful area of applied psychology.

Other attempts to achieve a clearer understanding of human behavior have led to an analysis of its component elements. No suggested list of such components has met with unqualified approval, and there has been endless discussion of the definition of terms. For example, I suggest that it would be helpful if we considered behavior as made up of habits, instincts, and intelligence or learning; but it has proved quite difficult to define these traits or characteristics without realizing that they overlap and are not clear-cut. However, the concept that behavior is made up of these three elements is a useful one.

Habits are forms of behavior that have become permanent or settled by persistent repetition. Many of our peculiarities of speech and gesture are habit behavior. We think of drinking or smoking as habit traits. There is considerable agreement on the meaning of habits. But when we speak of man's instincts, we find great difference of opinion. What should be classed as instinct? Some authorities define instinct as a natural impulse or urge; they speak of the "urge" to preserve life, or the urge *toward* pleasure and *away from* pain or the urge to secure happiness. Other authorities, observing the complex type of instinctive behavior in the lower forms of life, define the word as "a congenitally organized pattern of behavior." These opposing views correspond to the differences between the introspectionist and the behaviorist in the field of psychology.

When we come to decide what part of behavior is instinctive as opposed to learned, the relationship of the two areas is far from clear. Man's ancestor, we believe, adjusted to his environment primarily by the functioning of his instincts. Slowy but surely his intelligence began to challenge the dominance of his instincts. In this struggle between instinct and intelligence our present civilization had its genesis. As Roderick Seidenberg puts it, "History is seen as a specific process of continuous conflict and dynamic change arising out of the ever varying relation between instinct and intelligence in the structure of our world."

Predicting Behavior

In spite of its seeming complexity, human behavior *is* predictable and understandable. It has a discernible pattern of development and is governed by its own internal logic. To discover the predictable elements in behavior requires an intensive kind of analysis. We should begin by learning its latitudes and its balance of forces in "normal" circumstances. With these guides, we are in a position to predict a course of behavior under a given set of circumstances.

Under certain conditions, such predictions become simple if we consider the actions of individuals as members of a large group. Then we can apply the mathematical laws of probability. In any given number of tosses of a coin, the probability is that heads will come up 50 per cent of the time and tails 50 per cent. The greater the number of tosses made, the closer the results will agree with these percentages.

Shortly after World War II, an interesting case of mass behavior on the part of millions of inhabitants of New York City was the subject of intensive investigation by the city water department. For some reason the water pressure began dropping off in the evening hours exactly on the hour and the half hour. The drop in the pressure was so precipitous and so consistent that it caused great alarm. The department selected a random sample of the city's population large enough to give reliable results, and subjected these people to the investigations of psychologists, sociologists, mathematicians, and detectives. It was conclusively established that between the hours of seven and ten in the evening, precisely on the hour and half hour, toilets were being flushed and a corresponding number of faucets turned on.

From the facts set forth here, you have probably already deduced the cause of the phenomenon. It was the advent of television. People left their sets for the kitchen and bathroom on the hour and the half hour, during the station breaks and commercials. Of course, it would be impossible to say with certainty that a particular person would visit the bathroom on the stroke of seven P.M. But the mathematics of the situation make it possible to guess that he might.

Even individual behavior can be predictable in certain cases—when the circumstances are known and understood. In Hong Kong there are certain individuals who, at certain times of the day, play Mah-Jongg for money. It can be predicted that they will win.

Why? Because it is traditional for health inspectors, after examining a restaurant, to drop into the back room for a fast turn with the Mah-Jongg tiles. In the entire history of the colony there has never been a case of an inspector losing.

Sometimes you will come upon an apparent suspension of the law of averages. Look for the facts behind it. There is a reason.

The predictability of mass behavior is a part of our daily life. For example, when we drive a car along the highway we stake our lives on the belief that we can predict the behavior of the drivers of the cars coming from the opposite direction. We wager our lives on the probability that not one of these drivers will suddenly decide to swerve in front of our car. Of course there exists the *possibility* that it could happen, but based on the probabilities of mass behavior, the event is not likely to occur very often. If this were not so, few of us would continue driving.

In the course of our life experience, we have formed many judgments on the basis of mass behavior and we apply them to many situations, without thinking. For instance, if you are traveling on a train and it comes to a sudden stop, you would think with assurance that the train had stopped because of some mechanical trouble, not because the engineer had left his post to pick flowers along the tracks. In other words, you would realize that the mechanical behavior of the train is *less* predictable than the human behavior of the engineer. As Sherlock Holmes remarked to Dr. Watson, "While the individual man is an insoluble puzzle, in the aggregate, he becomes a mathematical certainty.

You can never foretell what any one man will do, but you can always predict with precision what an average number of men will be up to. Individuals vary but percentages remain constant."

Many people involved in negotiation fail to utilize this type of working hypothesis as a convenient negotiating tool. I have sat down at the bargaining table with many lawyers, businessmen, and real estate operators. For the most part, they proved to be reasonably skillful, resourceful negotiators even though they may never have studied the elements of human behavior. They have had to rely upon their personal experiences, and from long years of practical bargaining they have acquired a remarkable comprehension of some of the skills and techniques involved in understanding others. These people say, "You can't argue with success."

However, I say that they are willing to settle for a poorer result than they are capable of obtaining. Learning by experience is a slow empirical process and can never lead to a broad knowledge of a subject. Individual experience may give you an adequate ability to negotiate, but it certainly can never give an insight into the wide range of possibilities that are available in a negotiating situation.

Some people recognize the inadequacy of their experience and attempt to broaden their outlook by studying the modes of behavior practiced by others while negotiating. Usually these other individuals they study are their adversaries in a bargaining situation. Benjamin Disraeli has said, "There are exceptions to all rules, but it seldom answers to follow the advice of an opponent." I would change the word "advice" to "example." In such instances an accurate appraisal is very difficult because the methods these people study are the very ones being employed to counteract their own actions or techniques.

The Why of People's Actions

Here are some of the psychological labels given to problems involved in understanding our own behavior and that of individuals with whom we must negotiate.

Rationalization. When a person rationalizes, he is interpreting a situation in a manner that will place him in the most favorable light. A character in Gilbert and Sullivan's operetta *The Mikado* rationalizes a lie by calling it "merely corroborative detail, intended to give artistic verisimilitude to a bald and unconvincing narrative." To avoid unpleasant feelings and bring about greater conformity with their inner expectations, people often "reconstruct" past events into acts favorable to themselves. They rationalize to justify their decisions, to give vent to their feelings, or to make themselves acceptable to their peers.

At the conclusion of a negotiation, who doesn't try to rationalize the results? We are all familiar with the fable about the fox who, try as he might, could not reach a tempting bunch of grapes. He consoled himself by saying, "Oh well, they were probably sour and so I did not really want them." Now, as a matter of fact, he wanted the grapes very badly but when he realized that he could not get them, he consoled himself, covered up his sense of failure and frustration by saying that he did not want them after all. He was kidding himself, he was telling himself a lie. A psychologist would say he was rationalizing.

Another form that this type of rationalization can take might be called reverse sour grapes. When people are rejected by the in-group, they quite frequently seek emotional revenge by accepting the in-group's standard of values and attempting to excel them. A factory worker denied the need of belonging becomes a "rate buster," producing more than the in-group has set as the maximum of production. Many a successful man has been driven by the same compulsion to "show them" that he is superior.

Projection. When a person attributes his own motives to other people, he is projecting. Frequently this is done quite unconsciously. For example, recently I was authorized to negotiate the purchase of a motel chain from a Mr. Edwards. In the course of the transaction, I asked Mr. Edwards if he used any outstanding technique for negotiating. Not realizing the possible advantage that I might gain by what he was telling me, he confessed that his sole technique, applicable to every situation, was to take advantage of the desire of all people to make money. He was projecting. He was ascribing to other people his own overruling motivation to make money out of any negotiation. Edward's method worked successfully in the majority of cases because it was based on a basic human need. However, in our negotiation it failed, and no agreement was reached. My client wanted the motel chain for its goodwill and the prestige of its name, and he valued his reputation and self-esteem more than the amount of money to be made.

Projection is one of the most common and most important ways

human beings perceive and think about objects in the external
environment. The process is usually (some say always) unconscious, in the sense that the individual does not know that he is
coloring and perhaps distorting his perception of external objects
and people by imbuing them with his own characteristics. Most
accounts of projection emphasize the point that people typically
tend to project their undesirable traits. A habitual cheater may
console himself with the reflection that everyone cheats. Bernard
Shaw is said to have remarked that the chief punishment of a liar
is that he cannot believe others.

Displacement. People often give vent to their anger or take
out their aggression on a person or object that is not the cause of
their difficulty. They seek a scapegoat. Typical is the husband who
comes home from the office after a good dressing down by his
superior. Loaded with suppressed emotions, he relieves his injured
feelings by kicking open the door to his home, spanking his children, and picking a fight with his unoffending wife. Throughout
history men have been led by unscrupulous individuals who play on
this weakness. Finding a scapegoat upon which to place the sins of
a people has been a popular "sport" from ancient times right
down to the present day. Unwarranted emotions in a negotiation
may merely be the result of displacement.

Repression. The exclusion from conscious thought of feelings
and wishes that are repugnant or painful to the individual is called
repression. The convenient "forgetting" of an unpleasant past
event or future duty is an example. Freud insisted that forgetting is
motivated, *not* accidental. Certainly repression is at work when a
person suddenly remembers a disagreeable appointment, but only
after the time for keeping it is passed. A good negotiator, however,
would know quite well that the other party did not want to
attend.

Reaction-Formation. People often repress strong, unacceptable
drives, then think and act in ways that are exactly the opposite of
these repressed drives. It should be borne in mind that the repression is entirely unconscious. In *Hamlet,* we have a famous example of reaction-formation. The Player Queen, in a ludicrous,
bombastic style, protests that she will never marry again if her
husband should die. Hamlet's mother recognizes the truth in
her much-quoted comment, "The lady doth protest too much,
methinks."

Self-Image. Every individual has an image of himself that he synthesizes from his aspirations, his experiences, and the evaluations of those who hold him dear. Many personal decisions are made either to protect the self-image or to enhance it. Therefore, if we can know how a man regards himself, we can make assumptions about his motivations and his reactions to future events. There is always the possibility, however, that he might not bring his entire self-image out in the open. Then we must arrive at a clearer picture of his self-image by studying his previous actions and experiences.

Role Playing. The kind of behavior shown in acting out a role is based to a great extent on previous experiences in life. A man who is called upon to act the role of a father and administer punishment to his young son will usually act the way his own father did, or even exactly the opposite. It largely depends on what his own boyhood conception of punishment was. Usually we have a fairly clear conception of what role we want to play, or perhaps we should say we *think* we have it. However, when in doubt, we work out a role that satisfies us by trial and error.

As if to make our task of understanding human behavior still more difficult, we are told by some psychologists that when two people, A and B, meet for a discussion, there are actually six different personality roles involved. For A has three separate personalities present: A_1, the person that A *actually* is; A_2, the person A *thinks* he is (his self-image); and finally A_3, the person that A *appears* to be. The same threefold personalities of course apply to B, making six altogether. Whatever its overall validity, this concept is useful at the negotiating table. There every person plays a different role, depending upon his function in the situation. Very often he plays more than one role. If we understand the role-playing approach to behavior, we realize that we are apt to be dealing with a multiplicity of personalities even in the simplest negotiation.

Rational Behavior. Some types of behavior are often called "irrational." However, behavior should not be referred to as irrational until the assumptions and premises upon which it is based are understood. Louis D. Brandeis once stated, "Nine-tenths of the serious controversies which arise in life result from misunderstanding, result from one man not knowing the facts which to the other man seem important, or otherwise failing to appreciate his point of view." Human beings act in accordance with their individual rationality. We tend to call an individual rational if he considers the possible consequences of each of the courses of action open to him; if he is aware of a certain preference order in the consequences; and if he chooses the course of action which, in his estimation, is likely to lead to the most preferred consequence. In other words, we understand the premises and the standards by which the individual acts. If we lack this understanding, then we might say his actions are irrational. But this is a misnomer. It is *our* understanding of his premises and preferences that we cannot rationalize. A party may "irrationally" fly into a rage, but below the surface this may be a rational strategy to make the other side believe his threats. "There's method in his madness."

The problem of defining rational behavior is further complicated because it depends to a large extent on the probable behavior of other individuals. In gambling, the rational individual is one who maximizes the utility expectation accruing to him. To achieve as much as possible of his expectation, he must take into account the efforts of all the other "rational" participants of the game, who are trying to do the same thing. All these factors show that rational behavior is not static but depends on many complex, changing elements—the individuals, their backgrounds, the behavior of the other people involved, the premises that each of the participants believe in, the whole structure of the situation. In the Need Theory of Negotiation, dealt with in subsequent chapters, we will see that certain "irrational," behavior makes good sense when its relation to the overall structure of the negotiation can be understood and taken into consideration.

These thoughts on irrational behavior bring to mind the story of a man whose automobile tire went flat just outside an insane asylum. When he got out to change it, one of the inmates stood inside the fence watching him. He removed the wheel lugs and carefully placed each one in the hub cap, which he put on the side of the road. While he went to get the spare tire, a car sped past, hit the hub cap, and scattered the lugs all over the road. Search as he might, he was unable to find a single lug. He stood there bewildered, not knowing what to do. At this point, the inmate who had watched the entire occurrence called him over to the fence. When he approached, the inmate said, "I would suggest that you take one lug off each of the other wheels and put them on the fourth wheel, drive to the nearest service station and buy some additional lugs to continue on your trip." The man naturally thought that this was a wonderful solution to his predicament. Then he was suddenly quite embarrassed. The inmate asked, "What seems to be the trouble?" The man answered, "I'm very upset—here you are on the inside, telling me, on the outside, what to do." Whereupon the inmate replied, "Well I may be crazy but I'm not stupid."

In this instance the behavior of the inmate of the asylum would be considered quite rational. Obviously the driver could not think that all of the inmate's thinking was irrational.

Failing to understand people's premises and calling their actions irrational is but one of the barriers people set up. All of us go through life setting up barriers of one kind or another. We erect obstacles to attaining objectives that could have great value for us, and we cling to these imaginary barriers—perhaps for a lifetime. The following story illustrates this point. A farmer put up an electrified fence around his pasture land. After the fence had been up about a year, the neighboring farmer complimented him on his wonderful fence, saying that he had noticed that throughout the entire year, the cows did not go anywhere near the fence. He went on to say that it was not practical for him because he could never afford the electric bill that such a fence must entail. The other farmer laughed at this. "Don't let that worry you," he said, "I turned the electricity off after the second day. Those cows never realized the difference."

Ask a group of kindergarten children how many of them can paint and they will all say that they can. Try a classroom group in their thirties and probably all will say that they haven't the talent or the skill to paint. These are merely barriers that they themselves have built. If they could free themselves from these barriers, they would act creatively. Negotiation calls for the handling of situations with as few self-constructed barriers as possible. This facilitates open-mindedness, which leads to creative applications. People who open themselves to more experiences will become more creative. I am not able to give an overall formula for behaving creatively, but I know some of the things that prevent creative activity. A person under great stress will rarely attempt creative work. He prefers to engage in purely routine matters. In the face of stress, or danger, or the strange and unknown, people tend to retreat to the familiar and to noncreative behavior. A person in a completely dark room often closes his eyes. The darkness that he feels when his eyes are closed is more familiar than the strange darkness he experiences when his eyes are open.

When a man commits himself in advance to a solution by saying, "This is the best way" or "This is the only way"—the door to a creative solution is locked. A better way may become evident—but the man with prefabricated notions will either be blind to it or, worse, will have worked himself into a position from which he cannot emerge.

When we consider all the tricks of the mind 'that research in psychology has unveiled to us, we begin to realize the difficulties involved in studying the art of negotiation from our own experiences or those of other people in relation to our own.

In former times, human behavior did not appear so complicated. Not long ago, reason was deemed capable of solving all problems. People were conditioned to believe that logic expressed truth and that actions were either logical or illogical. They believed, with Aristotle, that reason held sway over a hierarchy of human capacities, that reason was at odds with man's emotions. Now the dynamic psychologists have changed all that. They have shown that human behavior is not a contest between the two forces of reason and emotion, the head against the heart, but a result of the combination of the two, plus many other factors— such things as environment (physical and cultural), cumulative experiences, and chemical balances.

However, as we have seen, this complexity need not create yet another barrier to the understanding of human behavior.

It is essential to deal with elements that are common to all people, momentarily disregarding basic individual differences. By dealing only with similarities, we can also achieve a clearer understanding of human needs, the key to successful negotiations.

People *rationalize*; they *project*; they *displace*; they *play parts*. Sometimes they *repress* things or *react*; conform to *self-images*; and engage in *"rational" behavior*.

The experienced negotiator can look at a man across the table and make a pretty good guess about how he is acting and what is causing that action. But mankind is a lifelong study. The true negotiator never stops learning.

We are moving into the area of negotiation proper. On the

basis of our acceptance of the cooperative approach—and fortified by our knowledge of human behavior—we next come to the stage of *preparation*.

IV

PREPARING FOR NEGOTIATION

"Thinking is more interesting than knowing, but less interest-'ing than looking" Goethe.

If you know that within one month you will find yourself across the table from your negotiating opponents, how do you prepare for this face-to-face encounter? How can you foresee the strategy of the opposite side, and how can you prepare to cope with it? The answer is not a simple one. It may be summed up, however, in a phrase reminiscent of school days: *do your homework.* There are any number of life situations for which preparation is necessary. Negotiation is one of these. For successful results it requires the most intensive type of long- and short-range preparation.

"Know Thyself"

This preparation requires, first of all, intimate knowledge of yourself.

If you can be easily goaded to anger, you are very apt to be tricked into an unfavorable settlement because of your emotional state. People in an emotional state do not want to think, and they are particularly susceptible to the power of suggestion from a clever opponent. The angry person cannot instantly change direction, even if he finds that he has just made a ridiculous blunder. The excitable person is putty in the hands of a calm, even-tempered negotiator, a negotiator who has learned how to use emotions *only* for effect.

For these reasons a long-range preparation for negotiation must begin with a form of self-evaluation. It involves an intimate examination of your sense of values, your philosophy of life; it means, in a sense, taking stock of your intellectual and emotional makeup. The question may well be raised whether an individual can accomplish this soul-searching by himself. Sometimes this can be done only with professional help. The procedure resembles the techniques of psychoanalysis. The goal, however, is not the cure of a neurosis but the ironing out of any obvious personality defect, the ferreting out of hidden bias and fixed prejudice, and the elimination, in general, of those traits and quirks of the mind that interfere with your negotiating ability. The basic precept is: *know thyself*. As Polonius advises his son, "To thine own self be true."

How do you go about examining yourself? You must have the courage to ask yourself many disturbing questions, perhaps beginning: What, in general, do you seek in life? What do you want out of your business career? What do you want from *this* particular situation? Going from the general to the specific is by no means an easy task. As Lincoln Barnett has stated: you will be trying to transcend yourself and perceive yourself in the act of perception.

Somebody has likened the self-reflective process to the endlessly repeated image that we see of ourself when seated in the barber's chair between two mirrors. Hundreds of images of our face sweep out in a curve that stretches back to infinity. Perhaps each face in the long row is some particular aspect of our character that demands an examination. If we can ask each reflected face the correct question, then they will all fuse together into one complete, healthy personality. The problem of self-evaluation becomes still more involved if we imagine seeing our image reflected from two distorting mirrors—the distortion resulting, let us say, from our personality complexes.

Other long-range training for negotiation calls for the exercise of a variety of skills. You must have the patience and accuracy of a scientist in searching the literature of past experiments. You must combine the scientific attitude with the cunning of a detective in digging up facts and figures about your opposition. You should be able to apply the current teachings of psychology to predict what the other fellow will try to do. To solve a problem it sometimes becomes necessary and important to learn many new long-range skills, an important one being the art of listening.

My father learned the art of listening at a rather early age. When he was fourteen and thought he knew everything, an old relative took him aside and said, "George, if you want to have the same knowledge at twenty-one that you have now at fourteen, then continue to talk rather than listen, because if you continue to talk, you won't know any more at twenty-one than you know now." La Rochefoucauld states this another way: "One of the reasons that we find so few persons rational and agreeable in conversation is that there is hardly a person who does not think more of what he wants to say than of his answer to what is said." The skill of listening, concentrating on what was being said, as well as what is not being said, can prove to be enormously helpful in negotiations.

After you have completed your research, you must keep an open mind and always be ready to make changes in your appraisal of the situation. It is possible that some of the facts may require modification or that your approach must be changed. Lapse of time alone often tends to call for a change in strategy. Therefore it is important to be constantly on the alert for new developments.

It has been said that one never loses until one gives up. Consider the following example. In 1935 the "Nuremberg decrees" went into effect. By 1936 all borders of Germany were sealed to the Jews. Yet sitting next to me at a closing in 1955 was a real estate investor who had managed the almost impossible feat, not only of escaping with his life, but also of taking his life savings out of Germany. The passage of time did not dim his satisfaction and pride in telling the story of this feat. The essential elements were ingenuity and guts.

It was necessary for him to trade all of his holdings at a huge discount for United States registered corporate bonds. Ingenuity enabled him to contact an agent in Switzerland, who, he hoped, would register the bonds in the United States in the name of the new Jewish purchaser. He had committed his fortune to the oral promises of others. All of this accomplished, he had to take the next step. After memorizing the precious serial numbers, with "guts" he lit a match and made a small "bond fire." Paying the necessary bribery fee, he was permitted to cross the German border "penniless." When he arrived in the United ·States, he went straight to the office of the register agent for the corporation that had issued the bonds. He reported the destruction of the bonds and their serial numbers, and received replacements shortly thereafter.

Do Your Homework

An important phase of short-range preparation for negotiation is research. Research should be objective; objective not in the quality of the evidence you gather but in your attitude toward such evidence. There is a positive reason for amassing information. It amasses a wealth of material in your mind so that you may take advantage of any new development in the negotiation.

You should be prepared with every possible kind of information about the people with whom you are going to negotiate. When President Kennedy was preparing to go to Vienna for his first meeting with Khrushchev, he made it a point to study all of Khrushchev's speeches and public statements. He also studied all the other material available relating to the Premier, even including his preference in breakfast food and his tastes in music. It is doubtful if such intensive research would be required in most negotiating situations, but the extreme importance of President Kennedy's conference warranted this meticulous search for every detail concerning his protagonist.

An increasing need for facts in all areas today is causing a growing furor about such ideas as a "National Data Center"—a giant computerized "dossier bank" that could pull together all the scattered statistics about any American and make them available to those who needed them.

It is a distasteful idea to many, and yet the negotiator must sometimes subordinate his personal feelings about "snooping" to the exigencies of the negotiation process.

To utilize the information you obtain from research, you must rely upon your general fund of knowledge and experience. It is essential to examine the opponent's past history, inquire into previous transactions he was connected with, and look into every business venture or deal he has consummated. Also investigate any deals he has failed to conclude successfully. Frequently you will learn as much, or more, about people from their failures as from their successes. If you carefully analyze the reasons that a certain deal fell through or a negotiation failed, you will probably get a good understanding of how the opponent thinks, his method of operating, his psychological approach. All this will give you clues to his needs and prepare you to negotiate with him more advantageously. Consider what proposals he made, what counter-proposals he rejected and why, how flexible he was in the bargaining, how emotional was his approach.

You can obtain clues about the positions that business firms will take by studying some of their past transactions.

Sources like the following can prove helpful:

> Budgets and financial plans.
> Publications and reports.
> Press releases.
> Instructional and educational material.
> Institutional advertising.
> Reports of government agencies like the Securities and Exchange Commission.
> Officers' speeches and public statements.
> Company biographies in Moody's and Standard & Poor's.

Suppose you are studying an opponent's previous deal that involves the purchase or sale of real estate. The value of the tax stamps that were affixed to the recorded deed will tell the price at which the property was sold. Bear in mind, however, that there have been instances where an excess amount in tax stamps has purposely been used to attempt to hide the actual price of the property. Do not rely on one source. There are other agencies that will assist you in getting a fairly close idea of how much the property was sold for. Try to use more than one source for verification.

Merely by investigating a previous real estate sale, you can get an idea of what kind of man you are going to deal with. You can find out how long he held the property before he decided to sell it and how much profit he was satisfied to take. All these factors are useful in sizing up a prospective opponent. You can never know too much about the person with whom you will negotiate. In the words of Francis Bacon, in his essay *Of Negociating*:

> *If you would work any man, you must either know his nature and fashions, and so lead him; or his ends, and so persuade him; or his weakness and disadvantages, and so awe him; or those that have interest in him, and so govern him. In dealing with cunning persons, we must ever consider their ends, to interpret their speeches; and it is good to say little to them, and that which they least look for. In all negociations of difficulty, a man may not look to sow and reap at once; but must prepare business, and so ripen it by degrees.*

A trial lawyer's cross-examination of his adversary's expert witness should be more than a spur-of-the-moment inspiration. It must be prepared effectively. In New York State negligence cases, lawyers are required to submit the plaintiff to an examination by the defendant's doctor. No experienced attorney would let the client attend such an examination without him. When the attorney is in the doctor's office, he may have a chance to look at the doctor's library. It is advisable for him to take note of books that may have subject matter dealing with his client's injury. At the trial a most effective cross-examination, worked out in advance, can be conducted by having the doctor admit that certain books are the outstanding authority in the field, and further having the doctor admit that he possesses a copy of the book in his own library. As a result of having carefully analyzed these medical books, the prepared trial attorney will have devised a cross-examination to test any doctor's mettle as to whether he is really a qualified expert.

In examining a person's library, you can gain useful information which will add to your store of facts about him: his present and past interests, hobbies, intellectual pursuits, even the extent to which he is able to follow a subject through.

Another quite effective method of short-range preparation is to check records of previous litigation involving the prospective opponent. (These are available through litigation reports, which may be bought.) In addition to finding out if there is any recorded judgment against him, it will prove useful to know all details about any lawsuits in which he was involved. A fruitful source of information is inquiries made of the people who have litigated with your opponent. An amazing amount of useful information can be obtained from these people. They invariably contribute some facts and opinions that are not found in the ordinary record. These same methods of approach can be employed, not only to investigate the party with whom you are going to negotiate, but also to learn more about somebody you may want to enlist on your side in the negotiation.

Almost 90 per cent of the information that seems most difficult to obtain can be gotten by a direct approach. Try sitting down with your telephone and asking questions. If you are attempting to locate a person, one of the simplest methods is to call everyone in the phone book with the same last name and state that you want to locate a beneficiary under a will. With this as a reward, it is a rare instance that you would not receive full cooperation.

A wife wanted to know whether her ex-soldier husband, newly returned from World War II, was using his postal box to receive love letters from a girl friend who lived in England. When she was informed by her private detective that during the previous week her husband had not received any letters from his girl friend, the wife was not fully satisfied. After all, how could she be sure? She insisted on knowing how the detective obtained his information. He reluctantly explained his method. He merely had someone call the post office each day, explain that he was the holder of such and such a box, and ask the clerk to look and see if a very important letter expected from England had arrived. In response to the inquiry, the clerk had each day answered in the negative.

The *Dictionary of American Slang* defines the phrase "to have someone's number" as "to know the hidden truth about another's character, past, behavior, or motives. . . ." This aptly sums up what you are trying to do in your immediate preparation for negotiation. You are trying to know your opponent, you are trying to "get his number." Indeed our era could well be called the "number age." We are saddled with numbers from the day we are born until the day "our number comes up" and we die. We have a Social Security number, dozens of credit card numbers, bank account numbers, brokerage account numbers, stock certificate numbers, passport numbers, telephone numbers, house and street numbers, check numbers, and any number of other numbers. In modern. society men receive more numbers than they know how to handle.

And since we all have numbers, it is easy to get information about any given individual. There are many organizations that specialize in gathering credit information and their charges are quite modest. Large corporations, especially in the retail field, spend as little as one or two dollars for a credit report on a prospective charge customer. Often a simple credit investigation will reveal a vast amount of information about the person with whom you are going to negotiate. This type of research is valuable, and one can sometimes save thousands of dollars' worth of time for a very nominal price.

In researching a situation, always examine and reexamine the rules. How can anyone understand a specific situation without knowing the rules applicable to that situation? How many people read the instructions and bulletins that go with every mechanical device they purchase or even with the medicines they buy? There is the story of the toy manufacturer who starts his assembling manual with: "When all else fails follow the instructions." This being the case, it is not surprising that people who attend an auction or a legal sale have not bothered to read the rules. Sometimes these rules are, unfortunately, learned from experience—usually a bad experience.

You may feel that you already know the rules applicable to your negotiating problem, that it is unnecessary to reexamine them. Then try a simple test. Cover the face of your wristwatch with your hand. Now think, are the numbers on the face Arabic or Roman numerals? Also, how many numerals? Uncover the face and check. Try the same test with a friend. As we go through life we look at the hands of the watch, noting their relative position, abstracting out the other details, never taking notice of the face. We do the same thing with rules. When we consider them, it is only in reference to the specific factual situation. It is therefore necessary to reconsider the rules with each new problem.

An outstanding illustration of this need to reexamine the rules was given by an associate who invited me to attend an auction of a surplus aircraft plant owned by the government. The General Service Administration had put the plant up for auction and it was, supposedly, to go to the highest bidder. Fred, my associate, and I discussed the relative value of the property and determined that we would offer $375,000 for the building and equipment. A hundred or more people had arrived at the auction before us, but Fred, by intuition, was able to look over the crowd, point out a group of three men and say, "There's our competition." He was absolutely right. Brokers and bidders in an audience behave differently. When the bidding began, we started with a bid of $100,000, and they countered with $125,000. We bid $150,000. When they had bid up to $225,000 Fred was silent and we left the auction. I was extremely puzzled; our final bid was supposed to be $375,000. But once outside, Fred explained to me that he read on the offering circular that, according to the rules of this auction, if the government did not feel that the price was high enough, they could reject it. Since we were the second highest bidder, the auctioneer would naturally contact us, tell us that the bid of $225,000 had been rejected, and ask us if we would care to make another offer. We could then counter with a higher price and at the same time ask the government for certain valuable concessions, such as taking a portion of the price in a mortgage. Within seven days this occurred just as if Fred had written the script.

Research supplies information to help anticipate the strategy of the impending negotiation. Such preparation should help answer questions like the following:

1. Are there any penalties involved in this negotiation, such as a penalty for bluffing, or a penalty for giving false information?

2. Have you recognized all of the interested parties to the negotiation?

3. Has anyone placed a time limit on the negotiation, or is there a natural time limit?

4. Who would like to maintain the *status quo* and who would like to change it?

5. What would be the cost of a stalemate?

6. In this negotiation, what will be the means of communication between the parties?

7. Can many items be introduced into the negotiation simultaneously?

By carefully exploring questions of this type, you will gain fresh insight into the strategy of the negotiation about to take place.

The Newer Methods

In addition to the traditional ways of preparing for negotiation, such as doing your homework and examining the rules, other methods have come into vogue fairly recently. These methods employ the techniques of *group drama* (the *psychodrama* and *sociodrama*), *brainstorming*, and the *conference*. At first glance such techniques may seem far removed from anything to do with negotiation. They were originated by psychologists or by the advertising fraternity. However, they are used to find the answers to problems, and in preparation for negotiation you also are seeking to solve problems. You want to know what the other fellow is going to say, what he is going to offer in response to what you say and do —in other words, what his thinking will be. The use of the group approach has proved to be a highly efficient way to get the answers to these questions. Group therapy and group methods of solving problems owe their efficacy to the power of suggestion and to the giving and getting of feedback. Solving problems through a group judgment has often proved superior to results obtained by individual judgments. This has been recognized in the advertising profession.

The method called *brainstorming* has largely superseded the ordinary conference in certain situations, such as originating a name for a new product or a slogan for a campaign. The method is essentially simple. Suppose that a problem has come up, or a new brand name is to be adopted. The usual practice would be to call a conference of the qualified executives in order to get their various opinions; then a decision would be made on the basis of what had been said. In a brainstorming session, a suitable group of people is brought together, with a secretary. The problem is presented in a clear and concise way. From this point on, the discussion and thinking aloud is permitted to move in any direction. Each person says whatever comes into his mind. No attempt is made to correct or evaluate any statements made, but the secretary takes down every word that is uttered, no matter how strange or outlandish it may seem. The entire transcript of what was said is then turned over to the top executive personnel for evaluation.

What is the theory behind this type of group meeting, and why should it produce results? It is believed that brain activity in a group becomes infectious. Ideas appear to grow by being ping-ponged back and forth. The informal atmosphere of the talk and the strong suggestive stimulus of the group thinking give a feeling of security and relieve inhibitions. Under the influence of group discussion, the individual's thinking is quickened and many fresh, original ideas are obtained that far excel those produced in a conventional conference.

Group psychotherapy, which originated with Freud, has been subjected to many refinements since its inception, and in recent years J. L. Moreno has made significant improvements in its application. Moreno uses groups of individuals to act together in a form of improvised play to solve individual problems. He calls this *psychodrama*. Psychiatrists use psychodrama to bring out hidden feelings, attitudes, frustrations, and emotions. In essence, the individual acts out different parts in the group setting.

This technique can be valuable in preparing for negotiation because it permits you to act out the entire negotiation before it takes place. At various times you can play yourself, or an adviser to your side. If you choose, you can assume the role of the other party, or his adviser. Indeed, where the circumstances warrant, it is a good idea to play every one of these roles. It helps you to see what lies before you in the coming negotiation and presents it much more vividly than if you merely talked about it. This method of selecting a definite role and acting it out with a group of other players gives you a chance to try something without the risk of failure. It permits you to bring into focus any important elements that you may have overlooked or ignored. It also permits associates to participate more fully and freely with each member of each side of the group. Furthermore, it facilitates making corrections in your preparation because it lets you put yourself in the other fellow's place. (The police use a technique of role playing when they attempt to reenact their concept of how a crime occurred.) On becoming an attorney, I was fortunate to work in the law office of Lloyd Paul Stryker, one of the outstanding trial attorneys of the day. In his book, *The Art of Advocacy*, Stryker discusses preparation for trial: "I often simulate the witness and ask one of my associates to cross-examine me and to unhorse me if he can. It is great exercise, in the performance of which I have often found that I did not do so well as I hoped. My failures and the reasons for them are then discussed, and I now ask my associate to change places with me and then I cross-examine him. From this, new ideas are developed while all the time the client is looking on and listening."

Before canonizing a saint, the Roman Catholic Church traditionally appoints a "devil's advocate," who is instructed to advance all the *negative* arguments, all the reasons why the person should *not* be canonized.

In another example, week after week during the football season coaches assign substitutes to act the role of the next opponent's star player. A substitute professional quarterback will find himself acting the role of one opponent one week, another the next.

There is an important difference between the "playacting" type of meeting and an ordinary *conference*. In brainstorming a group of people with specified knowledge, experience, and attitudes are called together. Their free and uninhibited participation in discussion can prove useful in solving a problem by group judgment. The individuals called for a conference, however, are not necessarily selected for their special knowledge or experience. A conference may be called for full discussion and fact finding. Guidance or leadership, an unimportant factor in group dramas, plays a vital part in the success of a conference. A conference is for communication, and the communication can be steered in any of three directions: upward, to solve problems; downward, to inform or instruct people; and horizontally, to coordinate or cooperate. Many useful things may emerge from a conference if open communication and a free flow of information are allowed. Certain problems are handled better by the use of the group drama technique, whereas others are dealt with more efficiently in a conference— although we can understand what Tavares Desa, Undersecretary of Public Information for the United Nations, meant when he said, "If you want to get a thing done give it to one man, if you don't want it done give it to a committee."

Group dramas give opportunities for self-analysis. A study of your own motivation and thinking often gives you clues to the probable point of view of your opponent. This gives you the chance to ask yourself exactly what you want from the forthcoming negotiation. A thorough exploration of this question will serve to clarify your thinking on acceptable solutions to the problems to be negotiated, and will also suggest possible compromises that might be made. The answers will not be in absolute terms, but will rather concern the degree of probability of the solution.

A Case History

These days, some of the most rigorous negotiation takes place within a corporation—between one department and another. No business is altogether frictionless. The executive who is trying to maximize the effectiveness of his own part of the operation sooner or later runs into conflict with other departments—and other executives who are also trying to be effective and look good in the process.

When this happens, skill at negotiations is essential to the manager. It can mean life or death for his career.

Let's take a typical case. Mantee, Inc. is a medium-sized company manufacturing a line of office equipment. The episode essentially concerns two men: Fred Jones, vice-president for engineering and design, and Lee Parker, vice-president for sales.

Mantee has begun to market a new machine, called the "500." It is not important to specify its exact function. The "500" was developed by Jones's department, which also maintains the responsibility for inspection and quality control. Parker's job is to sell the "500," along with the other products that Mantee manufactures. He is also responsible for the servicing of the equipment after it is sold.

When Jones agreed that the "500" was ready for marketing, he specified that it was not to be run at more than 1,300 units per hour. His staff was still working on modifications that could possibly double that output.

However, Jones has found out that a number of customers are running the machine at a much higher capacity. Subjected to this kind of stress, the "500" seems to have held up pretty well, but there have been some breakdowns in use.

Jones confronts Parker with this, and with other information he has learned. While Parker's salesmen are not *guaranteeing* the higher output, they also are not emphasizing that the equipment should not be run above 1,300. Parker feels that he must take full advantage of the potential of this new machine while he has an edge over competition. It isn't just a matter of selling the "500"; with the "500" as a "leader," Parker is better able to sell the whole Mantee line. Furthermore, Parker adds, breakdowns in service have not reached anything near an intolerable rate.

Parker is willing to take the responsibility, but Jones, thinking realistically, realizes that a widespread product failure would have an extremely bad effect on the company's position. It would also reflect upon Jones's reputation and certainly not enhance his career.

Mantee's president, in meaningful tones, has told Jones and Parker, "I am most anxious that you work it out between yourselves." In other words, if at all possible there is to be a negotiated settlement. A meeting has been scheduled a week hence at which the two department heads are supposed to "work it out."

Fred Jones determines that he is going to use that week to fullest advantage. But his first move is not a burst of activity. Instead, Jones sits at his desk, thinking. He contemplates himself and his relationships with the sales department.

Jones has to face the fact that these relationships have been spotty. And, he must admit, he has been partly responsible for the situation. Jones considers the sales department a necessary element of the company, but he feels superior to them. What do they know about the painstaking research and the delicate design that go into a masterpiece like the "500"? In a way it has always been a wrench to place a precision product in the hands of salesmen.

Jones faces up to this—and to other feelings. To his pride and ambition, for example. He has a personal reputation to uphold in the industry, and he does not want it to be jeopardized by a sales staff that is driving to meet quotas. Not the most admirable motivation—but there it is.

When Jones has spent adequate time reviewing himself and his own feelings, he turns his attention to his opposite number in the negotiation: Parker.

Lee Parker is a "nice guy." A hearty, outgoing type, he likes people to like him. Nevertheless he is a shrewd sales manager and a good handler of men. And he is ambitious. Jones has seen the other man in action enough to know that Parker would like very much to climb to the top in the firm. For one thing, Parker has always tried to find out as much as he can about Jones's operation, and to ingratiate himself with Jones and his people.

Now Jones proceeds to make further preparations. He calls in his second in command, Harry Watson, and gives Watson a research assignment. Watson is to find out all he can in a number of specific areas about Mantee's recent sales history: who are its biggest customers, the state of customer relations, the ups and downs of customer service, and so on.

What, Jones asks himself, are the overall realities of the situation? For one thing, any settlement must not just bring one department or the other out on top. It must convince the president that it is the best possible solution in the light of the company's short- and long-range growth. Any other answer will make neither Jones nor Parker look good.

But the burden is on Jones to change things. The *status quo*—with the salesmen permitting customers to run the equipment at the higher rate—is satisfactory to Parker. It does not satisfy Jones. So he must change it.

When Watson has completed his research, Jones calls all of his key men together and goes over Watson's findings. They "brainstorm" the problem. Some of the suggestions are pretty wild, but Jones is beginning to formulate a plan. He roughs out the plan and then gets together with Watson for a head-to-head session. Watson is encouraged to play "devil's advocate"—to advance all the arguments that they both know Parker will advance.

Fortified with this preparation, Jones is ready to begin putting together a strategy. Certainly he is ready to consider the assumptions that will control the bargaining.

Before returning to Jones, Parker, and the Mantee case, let us consider the assumptions, often hidden ones, that affect negotiation.

V

HIDDEN
ASSUMPTIONS

From the time we are born we begin to form assumptions. Hot things are painful; mother's arms are warm and comfortable. And, as we mature, we continue to acquire a freight of assumptions at an enormous rate. We could not live without assumptions. When we hand the store clerk our money, we assume that he will give us our merchandise and our change. When we send in a subscription to a magazine, we assume that we will receive it. When we get on a plane to Chicago, we assume that it will land at O'Hare Airport. If we had to question everything, and reason everything through, nothing would get done.

But periodically it is necessary for us to reexamine our supercargo of assumptions. Some are wrong, and must be discarded. Others need to be modified. Still others remain valid.

Assumptions are a vital part of negotiations. In entering a nego-

tiation, a man is severely handicapped unless he reviews his own
assumptions—and anticipates the assumptions of the other party.

A SOURCE OF MISUNDERSTANDINGS

Justice Arthur T. Vanderbilt advised trial lawyers that when
they open to a jury they have to bear in mind the "intellectual
environment" of their case and not be deaf to the "assumptions
of the age" in which they live and speak, for they are not talking
in a vacuum to men without previously formed opinions. They
cannot flout or ignore public opinion—an opinion that is made
up of accepted principles—even though they know that it may
often be no more than the rationalized prejudices of the times.

Albert V. Dicey, in *The Relation Between Law and Public
Opinion in England During the 19th Century* (New York: Mac-
millan, 1905) writes, "Above all, bodies of beliefs may generally
be traced to certain fundamental assumptions which at the time,
whether they be actually true or false, are believed by the mass
of the world to be true with such good confidence that they hardly
appear to bear the character of assumptions."

Few people realize what a large part of our beliefs are based
on unconscious, hidden assumptions. They are not easy to bring
out in the open and we frequently fail to recognize their existence.
Like the iceberg, nine-tenths of our assumptions lie below the
conscious level. Assumptions certainly are not learned, in the sense
that we learn mathematics. When analyzed, they prove to be odds
and ends of information, or usually misinformation, gathered during our lifetime, or dogmas that have their roots in emotional conflicts.

The scrutiny of some "domestic" assumptions can turn up surprising things. A husband was watching his wife as she prepared a
roast for the evening meal. After placing the roast on the cutting
board, the wife cut the first slice and dropped it in the refuse can.
"Why did you do that, dear?" the husband asked. "I don't
know," was the answer. "My mother always did it." The next time
he saw his mother-in-law, the husband asked if she always removed the first slice from the roast before cooking it. "Yes," was
the reply. "*My* mother always did it." So the husband, intrigued,
called up his wife's grandmother. That elderly lady explained,
"Oh, yes, I always removed the end slice from the roast because
the pan I cooked it in was too small."

The assumption that a long accepted procedure is valid—without any knowledge of the facts behind that procedure—can lead to meaningless and wasteful activity.

Hidden assumptions are difficult to subject to rational verification. If we make the open assumption that a certain chair will support our weight, we can test its validity by sitting on the chair. If it holds us, then our assumption was correct. If it breaks down, the assumption was false. We would be foolish to keep on repeating this exact same experiment with the same chair. We learn and revise our thinking by testing our assumptions or those of our opponent. It is therefore important to know when we are putting our weight on an assumption, known or hidden.

There is nothing wrong with making assumptions. The problem arises when we act and think as if the assumption is the absolute fact. If we know we are making an assumption, we can be prepared for the unexpected, we are less likely to assert our position dogmatically and, if proved wrong, less likely to be hurt.

As a simple example of a hidden assumption, suppose someone were to ask you what they call the fourth of July in Great Britain? You might be at a loss to give the correct answer because you had *assumed* that what was asked was, "What do they call Independence Day in Great Britain?" Unencumbered by any hidden assumption, you would give the correct answer. What else would they call the day that falls between the third and fifth of July but the fourth of July?"

Here is another illustration of a hidden assumption. If someone told you that he saw a beggar walking out of a ladies' room, would you be shocked? Why might you be shocked? Because your hidden assumption of the situation is that the beggar is a man. But he did not say so. It is your hidden assumption that has led you away from the facts.

How often do we assume we know all the facts? This example was popular a few years ago. On a cold January day, a forty-three-year-old man was sworn in as chief executive of his country. By his side stood his predecessor, a famous general, who fifteen years previously had commanded his country's armed forces in a war which resulted in the total defeat of the German nation. This young man was brought up in the Roman Catholic faith, and, after the ceremonies, spent five hours reviewing a parade in his honor and stayed up until three A.M. celebrating. Who is it? The facts given were

enough to make the average American immediately assume that it
was John F. Kennedy. But it was Adolf Hitler.

Our assumptions are a vital part of the human communication
system. We must use them continuously in sorting out and trying
to make sense of the millions of ambiguous stimuli that confront
us. We receive a communication, interpret it, and make a "first
guess," an assumption which we stay with until it is disproved.
As the Gestalt school of psychology puts it, to probe a hole we
first use a straight stick to see how far it takes us. We might para-
phrase this and say that, to probe the world, we use an assumption
until it is disproved. We should remember that a simple assumption is easy to refute. The hidden assumption, however, is difficult
to recognize and correct.

Very often a great deal of time is wasted in a negotiation because both sides have misunderstood the facts of the situation.
Perhaps the facts have become distorted because one or both
parties are in the grip of hidden assumptions without being aware
of it. One should always go beyond the mere words of the negotiator. To find the facts, look to the "outside world" instead of to
the words of the opposition. If facts are true they can be verified,
and verification leads to a solution and away from misunderstanding. Often the successful function of a mediator is merely to interpret and convey information accurately.

The negotiator must never forget that what he assumes is only a
guess or a probability, but if he acts as if the assumption is a certainty, he takes a calculated risk. Therefore, if you can spot the
"assumed certainties" of your opponent, you can use his calculated risk advantageously.

A negotiator who fails to understand the immediate situation
because he is influenced by a hidden assumption is often stuck
with the assumption as a fact throughout the negotiation. This
can prove disastrous. An opposing lawyer unfortunately found
himself in such a position at a lease closing. This was a conference
on an important and complicated lease. Every closing is different,
as is every life situation, and as such should be handled as a separate and unique matter. There are printed lease forms known as
the Real Estate Board Form Leases. They are considered "standard" forms and are used fairly frequently in routine transactions.
They contain a mass of conditions in fine print. Even a lawyer
who had practiced law for fifty years would not remember the sig-

nificance of each and every item in these forms. My associate in the conference told the opposition lawyer, "Here is the standard Real Estate Board Form Lease. You undoubtedly know it by heart, practicing as long as you have." By this remark he forced the opposition lawyer to assume a role. Instead of analyzing the lease as it applied to the present situation, the other lawyer dispensed with reading the standard printed form. He assumed that examining it would show his lack of experience. He acted out the role into which he had been manipulated, that of having to know every word of the "standard" lease. He passed over the major portion of the lease and spent the remaining time discussing some of the typewritten portions, which, compared with the printed sections, were insignificant. The hidden assumption had been used strategically to his disadvantage. In business, particularly in selling, we have all seen examples of men being "stuck" with assumptions.

Even the vaunted power of the computer to solve problems can be vitiated by a hidden assumption. This was illustrated at an international conference on communication. An outstanding computer expert was reporting on the difficulties experienced in feeding problems to the computer. His company had been employed to determine the proper distance that one automobile should travel behind the car ahead. The following information went into the computer: the reaction time of the motorist, the weather conditions, the nature of the road surface, the friction coefficient of the tires, the air resistance of the car, and so on. Taking all this data into consideration, the computer came up with the following formula: You should allow one car length for each ten miles per hour of speed; for example, at thirty miles per hour allow three car lengths between you and the car ahead; at forty miles per hour, allow four car lengths, and so on.

But, when the experts came up with this formula, they did not realize that they had a hidden assumption built into it. This only became evident when they went on a road test to try out the formula. Then it developed that as soon as they allowed a distance of four, five, or six car lengths between their car and the car ahead of them, cars traveling on the lane alongside them would pass, cut in front of them, and fill in the space they were trying to maintain. The hidden assumption that invalidated the formula was that cars would travel in a single-lane road and would have the road pretty much to themselves, a condition that did not check with reality.

A few years ago some computer men boasted that they had created a perfect chess-playing machine. Their computer was programmed to anticipate—and defeat—any game played against it by even the greatest masters in the world. At least, this was the assumption.

It worked a few times. Then a chess champion, who had studied the computer's previous games, sat down to face his electronic opponent. His opening move was to advance a rook pawn one square. Then he advanced the rook one square. These were wildly irrational moves. The computer's lights flashed, but no answering move was forthcoming. Since the assumption was that the human master would play logical chess, the device had not been programmed to combat the illogical game.

Dr. Sydney Lamb, speaking at a Yale conference on computers and the humanities, said, "The computer is not intelligent at all, but very stupid indeed, and that, in fact, is one of its great values— its blind stupidity." But it is scarcely an advantage when human beings build hidden assumptions into the computer's results.

Words themselves frequently embody hidden assumptions. Such words as "sunrise" and "sunset" helped perpetuate the old assumption that the sun revolved around the earth. People have a tendency to label everything prematurely, thus seriously limiting their ability to perceive reality. They also react as though the label describes all there is to say about the object to which it is applied. For instance, many people react to the label "contract" as though it could only be the name of a legal instrument. This is far from true. A contract may contain selling devices that have nothing to do with its legal implications. As an example, franchise contracts might make provisions for a volume of business far exceeding the amount that the franchise dealer is likely to earn. On seeing these wildly optimistic figures, the potential customer is likely to assume that this amount of business *will* be done.

S. I. Hayakawa speaks about a still more basic hidden assumption in language when he states, "Underlying our beliefs are unconscious assumptions regarding the relationships between language and reality—a set of assumptions based, among other things, upon not distinguishing between statements about language and statements about the nature of the world." The study of general semantics will help immeasurably in analyzing and dealing with assumptions of all kinds.

CATEGORIES OF HIDDEN ASSUMPTIONS

Making three categories of hidden assumptions can prove useful in negotiating: first, those we make about the *extensional* world, the physical world which exists outside the mind of a human being; second, those concerning our *intensional* world, the world which exists within the mind of each of us; third, the *other* person's *intensional* world.

The first category, dealing with the *extensional* world, contains the largest and broadest areas of hidden assumptions. It concerns the environment, the time and space in which we live. We must try to verify, as best we can, the "facts" of the world around us, rather than accept a mental picture of the world. This was Galileo's intention when he attempted to verify the "logical" belief that a heavy object falls faster than a light one. When he dropped different size weights from the leaning tower of Pisa, he found that the assumption was wrong.

Most views of the outside world are based upon assumption, hidden or known. We must therefore subject these assumptions to continued verification.

Language is essential in representing the outside world to each of us. It can, however, be misleading in that its structure tends to force us to view the world as having only two values, black or white, good or bad. This is, unfortunately, the viewpoint of Marxian dialectic, and it is not helpful in understanding the world today. The world might be considered as made up of an infinite number of shades of gray, merging successively into one another. It is the great variety of values, the constant flow and change of ideas, that imparts splendor and vitality to our concepts of environment. Assumptions about the extensional world—encouraged by a strict language structure—can lead us to believe that there are absolutes. As such they would not be subject to any further verification. With this in mind, Harry Maynard warns us to beware of the hardening of our categories. The world is a "process," not an unchanging "group of things."

In the realm of the intensional world, we must be careful to realize that our inside world is only a picture of the outside world. We tend to make assumptions about our emotions and thinking. These can confuse us so that we fail to make the distinction between "I *feel* that . . ." and "I *think* that . . . ." The result is that feeling that the truth may be thus-and-so becomes transformed into thinking and believing that it is the case.

The ability to anticipate the other fellow's assumptions can lead to spectacular results in business. Not many businessmen try to circumvent the government legally by anticipating its assumptions, although many of them dream of finding a legal loophole in the regulations to which they are subject.

However, sometimes such schemes come to fruition—and they become classic stories.

The hundreds of years behind the U.S. Customs Authority make it virtually impossible to create a plan to get around customs regulations—and still remain within the law. But one importer did it. He did it by means of a careful study of the regulations—and by anticipating certain assumptions that the customs people would make.

Ladies' French leather gloves carry a high import duty, which makes them exceptionally expensive in the United States. The importer in this story went to France and bought 10,000 pairs of the most expensive leather gloves. Then he carefully separated all of the pairs of gloves and made a shipment of 10,000 *left-hand* gloves to the United States.

The importer did not claim this shipment. Instead, he allowed it to stay in customs until the period for claiming them had expired. When this happens, the customs branch puts the unclaimed merchandise up for auction—and this they did with the entire shipment of 10,000 left-hand gloves.

Since a batch of left-hand gloves was valueless, the only bidder on the lot was an agent of the importer. He got them for a nominal sum.

By now the customs authorities were aware that something was up. They alerted their men to be on the lookout for an expected shipment of *right-hand* gloves. They weren't going to let the importer get away with his scheme.

But the importer had anticipated this. He also anticipated that the customs men would *assume* that the shipment of right-hand gloves would arrive in one bulk lot. So he packaged his remaining gloves in 5,000 boxes, two right-hand gloves per box. He counted on the probability that a customs official would assume that, of two gloves in a box, one was a right-hand and one a left-hand glove.

The gamble worked. The second shipment passed through customs and the importer only paid duty on 5,000 pairs of gloves—

plus the small amount paid at auction to claim the previous shipment. Now he had 10,000 pairs of gloves in the United States.

The impressions we have absorbed over the years shape our
judgments and create bias. Therefore we must realize that ideas
do not have the same meaning for other people that they may
have for us. We must make the distinction between our intensional world and the other person's intensional world. Without
understanding the difference in points of view and interpretation,
we would be bound to feel that any settlement in a negotiation
would have to be based upon *who is right*. This is not productive.
With compromise as a goal, and with due regard to the nuances
of meanings, there are an infinite number of solutions available,
ranging from the almost positive to the almost impossible.

Here let us comment for a moment on a sophisticated and sometimes dangerous assumption—namely, that you are always *aware*
of your own hidden assumptions.

Some years ago I conducted a class in general semantics. In order
to demonstrate the hidden assumption to the students, I would
hold up what appeared to be a pencil and ask the class to tell me
facts—not assumptions—about the object I was holding. Students
would call out that the object was a pencil, that it was made of
wood, had lead inside, and so on. Then I would bend the object,
showing them that it was made of rubber—and that all their
"facts" were really assumptions.

A year or so after conducting this class, I myself attended a
seminar given by Dr. Bontrager of the Institute of General Semantics. During the seminar, Dr. Bontrager held up an object re-
sembling a pencil and asked his audience to write on an index
card the *facts* about this object. I wrote that the object appeared
to have six sides, appeared yellow, and so on. I concluded with the
statement that I, too, had used a rubber pencil to illustrate the
same point to my students.

After the cards were collected, Dr. Bontrager dropped the
"pencil" toward his desk. Instead of bouncing high, it gave a metal-
lic ring. The "pencil" was made not of rubber, but of steel.

We sometimes place ourselves at a great disadvantage with hidden assumptions about other people's motivations and actions. For
one thing, these assumptions about the intensional world of others
are colored by our own views. St. Paul gave us a beautiful example

of this when he said, "Unto the pure all things are pure." Our assumptions about others often take on an unreal quality. Instead of listening to what other people are saying, we indulge in wishful hearing. We assume, without any basis in fact, that they have said certain things. Sometimes we go so far as to make assumptions about what a person is going to say before he has had a chance to say it. We interrupt, present our version of what he is about to say, and never give ourselves the opportunity of hearing what he might have said. Thus we deprive ourselves of valuable information. When listening to our opponents we must realize that our view of the world is a personal one, that our value judgments are personal judgments, that our moral concepts are valid for us alone.

The hidden assumption plays a considerable part in all phases of business negotiation.

Let's return to the example introduced in the preceding chapter. The problem at Mantee, Inc. is whether or not the sales department should be allowed to continue selling a new piece of equipment—the "500"—without stipulating that it must not be run at more than 1,300 units per hour. Fred Jones, vice-president for engineering and design, has been instructed to "work it out" with Lee Parker, the vice-president for sales. In other words, Jones is to negotiate this matter with Parker.

Fred Jones has already made certain preparations for the negotiations by sitting down to think about the assumptions involved in the situation—his own assumptions, and Parker's.

It's not easy, but Jones makes a careful review of his own assumptions. Some of them seem obvious—at first. "I'm trying to do what I think is best for the company," Jones thinks. Then he examines that statement. He has to admit, after some thought, that, while the statement is not a false assumption, it can bear some modification. Sure, Jones is trying to do what's best for the company. But he is also thinking of his own career and his own reputation. His motives are not purely altruistic.

Jones reviews his assumptions about the coming negotiation. And he finds that, upon review, at least three of these assumptions are questionable.

He has assumed that Parker, the sales manager, is interested only in equipping his men with the most attractive possible sales story. But is that really so? Parker is a complex man—and his motivations may be more complex than such an assumption would allow for.

Then Jones finds he has been preparing his case on the assumption that the "500" is quite unreliable at the higher capacity. True, it has broken down sometimes when operated at this speed—but Jones decides that he cannot make so facile an assumption without further information.

As another example, Jones has been assuming that *all* expertise on matters of design and engineering lie within his department. The responsibility lies there, yes; but is it possible that people outside the department could make a contribution? Salesmen—or even customers? Jones concludes that his feeling about the expertise of his department is not necessarily a valid assumption on which to go into a negotiation.

After going over his own assumptions with a fine-tooth comb, Jones then tries to anticipate the assumptions that Parker will act on. (He must make the assumption that he *can* anticipate some of these—but he must also be aware that he may be wrong.)

In Jones's view, Parker is likely to assume that the engineering department has no interest in, or knowledge of, Mantec's sales history and problems.

Furthermore, Parker probably thinks that the theory-minded design people are vague about the current performance of the "500" in the field. Parker will assume that his department, which is on the "firing line," has harder information.

Then also, Parker may well assume that Jones is interested *only* in forcing the salesmen to stress the limitations of the equipment. Under that assumption, Parker will marshal his heaviest artillery to combat the requirement.

When he has thoroughly considered his own assumptions—and the anticipated assumptions of his opponent, Parker—Jones is better equipped to put together a strategy.

We must be constantly aware of the possible effects of hidden assumptions on negotiation. This applies to our opponent's hidden assumptions as well as our own. For example, suppose an opponent begins arguing with such heat and vehemence that you recognize his irrational emotional involvement. Do not allow him to push your emotional buttons and cause you to react. Work with him, as a judo specialist would, by not opposing force with force, or as a tug boat that docks an ocean liner. It does not just tug at the line but gradually takes up the slack and then applies even pressure. Continue to try to understand and relate to the "irrational" emotional involvement. After some effort, enough outside facts may become available to uncover a possible hidden assumption.

The artful negotiator will then be able to utilize the "facts" to the satisfaction of all.

VI

WHAT MOTIVATES US?

The satisfaction of needs motivates virtually every type of human behavior. A detailed list of these needs would be infinitely long, and even the attempts to devise classifications can result in an unwieldy number of subdivisions. These classifications do not show how needs overlap. Any such classification can only give a still picture of a living, changing process. When preparing for negotiation time permits us to study only the broad categories that deal with the essential and predictable.

Professor Abraham H. Maslow of Brandeis University, in his valuable book *Motivation and Personality* (New York: Harper & Row, Publishers, Inc., 1954), presents seven categories of needs as basic factors in human behavior. These provide a useful framework for studying needs in relation to negotiations.

Here is Maslow's list:

1. Physiological (homeostatic) needs.

2. Safety and security needs.
3. Love and belonging needs.
4. Esteem needs.
5. Needs for self-actualization (inner motivation, to become what one is capable of becoming).
6. Needs to know and to understand.
7. Aesthetic needs.

Physiological needs are common to all members of the animal kingdom. Their goal is satisfaction of biological drives and urges such as hunger, fatigue, sex, and many more. The recently developed concept of homeostasis attempts to define this category of needs more precisely. *Homeostasis* refers to the automatic efforts of the body to maintain itself in a normal, balanced state.

An amusing story dealing with a homeostatic need is told about a financial magnate who lay stretched out on his death bed. He was under an oxygen tent. At his side stood his loyal subordinate, tears streaming down his face. "Do not grieve," whispered the expiring tycoon, with considerable effort. "I want you to know that I appreciate your faithful services to me over the years. I am leaving you my money, my plane, my estates, my yacht . . . everything I have." "Thank you, sir," cried the subordinate. "You have always been so good to me all these years. If only there were something I could do for you in these last moments." "There is . . . there is," gasped the half-dead man. "Then tell me what it is," implored the faithful servant, "tell me!" "Stop pressing your foot so hard on the oxygen line!" the dying man managed to utter.

Homeostatic needs are undoubtedly the most dominant of all needs. A person may lack many things such as love, safety, or esteem; but if at the same time he is really thirsty or hungry, he will pay no attention to any other need until his thirst or hunger is at least partially satisfied. A starving man has no desire or drive to paint a picture or write a poem. For him no other interest exists except food. All of his capacities are devoted to getting food, and until he gets it, other needs are practically nonexistent.

It should be noted that the entire organism is involved in the gratification of a need. No one says, "My *stomach* is hungry," but rather "*I'm* hungry". When a person is hungry, his whole being is involved, his perceptions change, his memory is affected, and his emotions are aroused by tensions and nervous irritability. All of these changes subside after he has satisfied the hunger need. When one group of needs has been somewhat gratified, however, another set becomes the motivating force.

After the physiological needs are taken care of, the organism is primarily concerned with *safety*. It becomes a safety-seeking mechanism. As with the hungry man, so with the individual in quest of safety. His whole outlook on life is affected by a lack of safety. Everything looks less desirable to him than the achieving of the goal of safety. Safety needs are more easily observed in children, because adults in our culture have been taught to inhibit any overt reaction to danger. But anything unexpected and threatening makes the child feel unsafe, and changes its world from bright stability to a dark place where anything can happen. A child feels safe in a predictable, orderly world; he prefers an undisrupted routine. He tends to feel safer in an organized, orderly world that he can count on and in which he has his parents to protect him against harm.

Adults in our society seldom come face to face with violence, except in war. They are safe enough from such perils as wild animals, extreme climate, slaughter or massacres. However, the need for safety expresses itself in seeking the protection and stability afforded by such things as money in the bank, job security, and retirement programs. Though human beings no longer live in the jungle, they need protection against the dangers that confront them in the ominous "jungle" of economic competition.

After the physiological and the safety needs have been reasonably gratified, the next dominant need to emerge is the *craving for love and affection*. This longing for friends, or a sweetheart, or family, can take complete possession of a lonely individual. When he was starving or threatened by danger, he could only think of food or safety; but now that these needs have been taken care of, he wants, more than anything else in the world, to be loved. He hungers for affectionate relations with people in general, for a place in his group. In our culture, it is just these needs and cravings that are most often left unsatisfied. Feelings of not being loved, of rejection, of "not belonging" are at the root of most cases of maladjustment and the more severe neuroses. This need for love must not be equated with sex. Admittedly it is a component of the sexual drive, but sexual behavior has many facets and is primarily a physiological urge.

Next in the hierarchy of basic needs is the need for *esteem*.

Actually it is a plurality of needs, all of the same general character. These needs can be divided into two categories. First and foremost is the desire for freedom and independence. Coupled with this is the need for strength, competence, and confidence in the face of the world. The second division comprises the desire for reputation or prestige, the striving for status, domination, and the esteem of other people. Satisfaction of esteem needs helps a person to feel useful and necessary in the world. The most healthy self-esteem is based on respect from others that is deserved, not on unwarranted adulation.

Research and experience continually demonstrate the power of esteem in motivating human beings. Studies of individuals at various levels of the business structure have attempted to find out what makes people feel good about their jobs. The strongest and most lasting "good" feelings come from learning and growing on the job, expanding one's competence, increasing one's mastery, becoming recognized as an expert.

Studying the motivation of salesmen, the Research Institute of America has reached similar conclusions. Many salesmen may respond, when asked casually, that the only thing that moves them is money. However, *self-approval* and *social approval* often motivate salesmen to even greater efforts. The pride of craftsmanship involved in making a tough sale—and the possibility of being recognized by other salesmen as a "professional"—spur a man on when the additional money is of relatively little importance.

Even assuming that all the foregoing needs have been adequately satisfied, the individual may still be discontented and restless. What need does he now seek? Most people are not happy unless they are working at something that they feel they are fitted for. A musician wants to make music, an artist wants to paint, everyone would like to do the kind of work that he can do and enjoys doing. Unfortunately this is not always his lot, but insofar as he attains this goal he is at peace with himself. This almost universal need has been termed by Maslow *self-actualization*. Broadly speaking, self-actualization embraces the desires and strivings to become everything that one is capable of becoming. This striving takes various forms and will differ from individual to individual.

In the normal person there exists a basic drive to seek out *knowledge* about his environment, to explore, to understand. We all are motivated by an active curiosity that impels us to experiment and attracts us to the mysterious and the unknown. The need to investigate and explain the unknown is a fundamental factor in human behavior. This *need to know and understand* presupposes a condition of freedom and safety in which this curiosity can be exercised.

Lastly, human behavior is actuated by certain cravings that might be called the *aesthetic* need. Some individuals actually get sick in ugly surroundings and are cured by removal to a beautiful setting. Naturally this longing for beauty is strongest among artists. Some of them cannot tolerate ugliness. But Maslow includes in the category of aesthetic needs the action of a man who "feels a strong conscious impulse to straighten the crookedly hung picture on the wall." Indeed, the need for order and balance is a basic part of all aesthetic expression.

These seven basic needs have been presented in a descending scale of importance. For most people and for most human behavior this fixed order holds true. However, it must not be regarded as rigid and it certainly does not apply to all people. (Any set of generalizations has its limitations.) Undoubtedly there are many individuals to whom self-esteem is much more important than love, just as there are creative people for whom the aesthetic need fulfillment is just as important as a more basic need.

Differences are related to the diversities of human personalities. It is a question of how an individual's personality has developed. A person who has been deprived of love in his early life sometimes loses the desire and ability to give and to receive love. Another factor that tends to change the fixed order of importance is the undervaluation of all needs that are completely satisfied. A man who has never experienced hunger will consider food as secondary to all his other needs.

Maslow pictures each successive need as emerging after a prior need has been satisfied. This is not to imply that one need must be 100 per cent satisfied before the next one takes over, nor that each emerging need shows up suddenly like a jack-in-the-box. Usually the previous need is only partially satisfied before the emergence, bit by bit, of a new-felt need. Most people are partially satisfied in all their basic needs and, at the same time, partially unsatisfied. For example, if the safety need is only 10 per cent satisfied, then the next ranking need, the craving for love and belonging, will not yet emerge. However, if the safety need becomes satisfied to a greater extent, perhaps 25 per cent, then the next need will begin to appear in a small way, perhaps 5 per cent; and as the safety need approaches 75 per cent of satisfaction, the love and belonging needs may emerge 50 per cent. This overlapping of one set of needs with the next set, and the constant shifting of emphasis on what a person wants, preclude a state of complete satisfaction of any basic need. Indeed, people seeking to satisfy their needs try to avoid physical discomfort, shun the unsafe, appeal for understanding, abhor anonymity, dread boredom, fear the unknown, and hate disorder.

To sum up, an individual's existence is a constant struggle to satisfy needs; behavior is the reaction of the organism to achieve a reduction of need pressures; and behavior is directed to some desired goal. Our objective is to employ these facts about human needs in successful cooperative negotiation.

VII

THE NEED THEORY
OF NEGOTIATION

Needs and their satisfaction are the common denominator in negotiation. If people had no unsatisfied needs, they would never negotiate. Negotiation presupposes that *both* the negotiator and his opposer want something; otherwise they would turn a deaf ear to each other's demands and there would be no bargaining. This is true even if the need is merely to maintain the *status quo*. It requires two parties, motivated by needs, to start a negotiation. Individuals dickering over the purchase and sale of a piece of real estate, a labor union and management bargaining for a new contract, or the directors of two corporations discussing the terms of a proposed merger—are all seeking to gratify needs.

What these needs are has been explored in the preceding chapter. This information can be put to use in the quest for successful negotiating techniques: knowledge of the Need Theory permits us to find out what needs are involved on both sides of the bargaining table. The theory goes further: it guides our attention to the needs and varieties of application that actuate the opposition and shows how to adopt alternative methods to work with, or counteract, or modify our opponent's motivations. These needs, as we have explained, arrange themselves in a definite order of importance. The Need Theory enables us to determine the relative effectiveness of each negotiating technique. Moreover, the Need Theory gives us a wide variety of choice for our affirmative or defensive use. Knowing the relative strength and power of each need, we can decide on the best method of dealing with it. The technique that deals with the more basic need in each case will probably be more successful. The more basic the need, the more effective it will be as a gambit.

At this point, let us raise a "devil's advocate's" objection. Needs are often intangible. People who are satisfying needs act on the basis of emotion—not reason. Since this is the case, isn't it futile to attempt to offer a highly structured theory of negotiation? That question has undoubtedly been partly responsible for the lack of such a theory up to this time.

The answer to the question is *no*. Let us consider religion as an analogy. People are emotionally involved in religion, yet theology need not be unsystematic. On the contrary, although theology starts with an "act of faith," it is one of the most ordered and systematic disciplines we have.

A theory of negotiation, just like any theory of theology, must take into account relative strengths, alternatives, and multiple choices.

The Need Theory provides such a structure.

THREE LEVELS OF NEGOTIATIONS

In the Need Theory of negotiation, I have divided the different areas of negotiation into three main levels:

1. Interpersonal—negotiation of individuals.
2. Interorganizational (excluding nations)—negotiation of large organizations.
3. International—negotiation between nations.

It should be noted that organizations of any type cannot act by themselves, independently of people. They must act through people. Remember this when you are dealing with people acting on behalf of organizations. You can recognize two active levels of needs: the level of the organization's need, and that of the negotiator's personal needs.

Individuals, through identification, often transcend the boundaries of their own need structure and mentally become part of a larger organizational level group. Thereafter, in certain cases a less basic need of the group—for example, esteem—will take precedence over a more basic need—safety, for instance. The great majority of people in most nations do not want war, but their identification through nationalism permits them to be persuaded and propagandized into conflict and thereby to put their safety in jeopardy. Therefore we should not be misled into thinking that the hierarchy of the need structure does not hold true when an individual willingly risks death (safety need) for national honor (esteem need). It would appear that the esteem need in such instances is taking precedence over the safety need. However, because of identification, this is not the case.

VARIETIES OF APPLICATION

The Need Theory is applicable at all levels of approach. When closely analyzed, the techniques of negotiation under each need are seen to repeat certain forms, called the varieties of application of the need. I have divided them into six groups or categories.

The following variety of applications are placed in an order corresponding to the amount of positive control that we may ordinarily have over each application in a particular life situation. In other words, a negotiator has more control over *his* working for the opposer's needs (1) than letting the opposer work for his needs (2), and so on down to (6), which is the least controllable. The six varieties of application are the following:

1. Negotiator works for the opposer's needs.
2. Negotiator lets the opposer work for his needs.
3. Negotiator works for the opposer's and his own needs.
4. Negotiator works against his needs.
5. Negotiator works against the opposer's needs.
6. Negotiator works against the opposer's and his own needs.

Examples of the variety of applications at the various levels of approach will be presented in detail in Chapter X, "Life Illustrations." The categories are enumerated here to show how the

Need Theory enables the negotiator to utilize a multitude of choices in bargaining. Depending on his needs and how he has gauged the needs of his opponent, he can select from the six varieties of application the one or more that he deems best suited under the circumstances at the appropriate level.

The more alternative ways you have of handling a negotiating situation, the greater will be your chances of success over people who use only two or three methods again and again. Most people have a tendency to use the same methods repeatedly because they are based on their past experience. A new situation or problem does not ordinarily suggest a new method of solution to the limited negotiator. Also, people have trouble transferring a thoroughly familiar technique from one field of operation to another. A very prosperous ticket broker in New York City had grown rich selling tickets to hit Broadway shows at illegally high prices. To get the tickets, he had to pay "ice" to the theater managers. ("Ice" is the term for an under-the-table payment for each ticket.) Suddenly the broker had to have certified copies of his birth certificate within two days. The city records department told him that it would take two weeks. He was at a complete loss until someone suggested that if he slipped the department clerk "a few bucks" he would get faster service. He had never thought of transferring his successful technique outside of the theater.

The Need Theory shows the probable order of importance of negotiation maneuvers. Therefore it will give the negotiator a wide choice of methods to use in achieving a solution. Remember, the more basic the need you are able to deal with, the more probable becomes your success in negotiation. If the opposer uses a maneuver involving a less basic need, then you should deal with a more basic need and thus enhance your chances for success.

The method you decide to employ in negotiation is an effort to gain an advantage. Webster's Collegiate Dictionary defines gambit as "a chess opening in which the first player sacrifices a pawn or a piece for advantage in position." This so aptly conveys the nature of the Need Theory methods of negotiation that such maneuvers will be referred to as gambits. In negotiations no gambit is absolutely pure and simple. It frequently may involve more than one need, more than one variety, and more than one level. Sometimes classifications may vary because the same thought is emphasized in a different way. For example, 32° F. can be defined either as the melting point of ice or as the freezing point of water. Both points are the same. However, we use one or the other, depending on our interest or application.

Similarly, the Need Theory of negotiation is not limited in scope or form to the interpersonal. It holds true for all patterns of negotiating situations and can be applied to every level of approach from the smallest groupings to the largest. The following anecdote illustrates how the need of an individual can appear to correspond to the need of a nation.

During the 1930's Great Britain was in great financial difficulties. The Chancellor of the Exchequer did not know which way to turn and was on the verge of a nervous breakdown. On the advice of his doctor he went to Florida for a complete rest. Day after day he reclined in a beach chair, trying to regain his health. Gradually he began to feel better and started to take an interest in his surroundings. Sitting next to him was an alert-looking man in his middle forties who kept receiving a constant stream of visitors. The Chancellor could not help overhearing scraps of the conversation, which revealed that each visitor was consulting the man on some business problem, asking his advice, and usually departing with a satisfied expression on his face.

The evident respect shown for the man's business judgment prompted the Chancellor to inquire at the hotel about his identity. He was told that his neighbor on the beach was a famous New York accountant, well known for his ability to solve financial problems. The Chancellor made a quick decision. He engaged the accountant for a "very important mission, no questions asked" and explained that further details would be given him in London. There the Chancellor set forth all the financial troubles of the British Empire that were crying for a quick solution. After listening attentively, the accountant suggested that all the ledger books and other financial records be brought to a room of the Treasury and that he be permitted to study the problem.

The accountant remained locked in the room for seven days and seven nights. At the end of the period he asked that the King come and confer with him. Left alone with the King, the accountant said, "Your Majesty, I have carefully examined the books of the British Empire and my firm advice to you is that you put Canada and Australia in your wife's name."

In the eyes of the accountant the needs of an insolvent individual and of an insolvent nation were identical: to prevent assets from falling into the hands of creditors.

APPLYING NEED THEORY

The Need Theory in all its ramifications can be perceived in each negotiating situation. By applying this theory, you can trace the relationship between the tactics used in a negotiation and the needs involved. To get a clearer picture of how the Need Theory runs like a thread or leitmotiv through every negotiation, consider several diverse examples.

First is a negotiation that dates back to the fifth century B.C., when the Athenians were about to attack the Nelians. Thucydides, in *The Peloponnesian Wars*, Book 5, gives the speech the Nelian Ambassador made to the Athenians:

> *We, too, must tell you what our interests are and, if yours and ours happen to coincide, we must try to persuade you of the fact. Is it not certain that you will make enemies of all the states who are at present neutral, when they see what is happening here and naturally conclude that in the course of time you will attack them too? Does not this mean that you are strengthening the enemies you have already and are forcing others to become your enemies even against their intentions and their inclinations?*

The argument is addressed directly to the safety need of the Athenians. If they attack, they will stir up neutral states against them and they will be less safe than if they refrain from an attack. This type of appeal is considered under the safety need (letting the opposer work for his need) in the Need Theory of Negotiation.

Our next example of the use of th Need Theory is taken from an article in the *New York Herald Tribune*, written by Claude Lewis, entitled "Why There Was No Trouble in Newark." Without going deeply into the merits of the problem, let's see how it illustrates certain aspects of the Need Theory.

In August 1964, serious rioting had broken out in the streets of New York's Harlem. There was similar trouble in Rochester, followed by rioting in Jersey City, Paterson, and Elizabeth, three cities that were, in many ways, smaller Newarks. Newark is a heavily industrialized city with a population about half black, many clustered in the Central Ward. There were poverty, poor housing, and plenty of discontent. Everybody fully expected that rioting would break out in Newark at any moment; but it did not materialize. Why? Because, as Lewis says, "The Mayor's strategy was unique in Newark—and was uniquely successful."

The Mayor had made it a practice to keep in close contact with the leaders of the black community at all times. He made frequent visits to the Central Ward, the potential trouble spot. Through his consultations with the religious and civic black leaders, he was fully informed of the mood of the black community and well aware of black grievances. With riots and unrest flaring up in the cities around Newark, it needed just a spark to start an explosion. When a free-lance group of picketers from outside the city decided to hold a rally in the predominantly black section, the Mayor knew he had to act swiftly to head off trouble. He sent telegrams to over ninety community leaders. Within three hours, eighty-six representatives of city-wide organizations were in his office conferring on the best course of action. They turned the proposed rally from a potential riot to a peaceful drive for black voter registration. The Mayor's policy was successful because he worked for the esteem need of the blacks and for their need to belong, to be a part of the community, to find a place in the group life. Throttling these needs by banning the rally would have undoubtedly led to an explosion of violence.

Now let's compare what happened in 1964 with what was done— or *not* done—during the summer of 1967.

A new medical school had been proposed for Newark. All agreed that this was a worthwhile project—but a site had to be found. The chosen site involved the tearing down of many slum dwellings.

At meetings before the city boards in April, May, and June 1967, the people of the slums protested vehemently. Before the project was completed, the city fathers were told, "blood will run in the streets of Newark."

At the same time the Secretary of the Board of Education decided to resign. The sizable black community wanted to have a say in the naming of his successor. This demand was being ignored by city officials.

Then, on July 12, 1967, the fuse was lit. John Smith, a black cab driver, was arrested. He had been driving after his license had expired. Some felt that Smith had been handled roughly by the police. In any event the arrest touched off four days of rioting. People were killed; a thousand stores were wrecked or damaged; there was a loss of $10 to $15 million; there were 1,426 arrests.

In 1964 ingenious communication and negotiation had prevented violence. In 1967, for some reason, the greater possibilities for negotiation were ignored.

As a last example of the Need Theory in negotiation, let us examine its connection with the General Motors strike of September 1964. On September 29, 1964, the *New York Times* carried a half-page advertisement sponsored by the United Auto Workers International Union. The heading, in large type, read: "Why the GM Strike?" with a subheading: "The Issue—More Dignity, Not More Money." At this stage of the strike the question of wages was not in dispute because General Motors had offered to meet essentially the same wage benefits as the Chrysler and Ford contract settlements, which contained the most attractive economic gains ever won by automobile workers in a single set of negotiations. The unsatisfied needs of the workers were much deeper and more basic than a matter of hourly pay. To quote from the advertisement, "The real depth of the resentment of General Motors workers is against the lack of decent treatment and the denial of human dignity at their work place. . . . Money is not the basis for the strike. The central issue is how General Motors treats its workers on the job." The union then listed the points in dispute on which General Motors had refused either arbitration or mediation:

> Minimum standards of humane and decent working conditions.
> Fair and reasonable production standards.
> Sensible and enlightened disciplinary procedures.
> Relief from excessive and arbitrary overtime work.
> Adequate representations to insure enforcement of the corporation's contractual obligations.
> Provisions to improve job security for workers.

These were the demands or grievances of the union. We present them here in order to search out the needs that they indicate and to test the Need Theory as it shows up in this negotiation.

Obviously the last demand for improved job security is distinctly a safety need, demanding satisfaction. In the other issues, there would seem to be a commingling of needs. Certainly the element of esteem is strongly indicated. There is also the worker's longing to have his labor regarded as worthwhile. He wants to feel that he is more than just a cog in the huge production machine. He wants more say in matters that directly affect him. He has a need for esteem and self-actualization.

Applying the Need Theory of Negotiation, we may say that the union is seeking to bring pressure to bear on General Motors by emphasizing the needs of the workers in the areas of safety, esteem, and self-actualization. Indirectly the union is suggesting that General Motors itself will satisfy its need for esteem by fostering better human relations in its dealings with the workers.

Now let's proceed to the question of *recognition* of *needs*.

VIII

HOW TO
RECOGNIZE NEEDS

The recognition of need is made easy by the fact that every negotiation, in the final analysis, takes place between individuals. This is true whether it involves two persons haggling over a small deal, large organizations bargaining over a merger or a labor contract, or nations negotiating a treaty. In every case, individuals are dealing immediately with individuals. The problem is to find out what needs they represent, either personally or as the representative of a group.

To know what your opposer is thinking and striving for, you must turn detective, you must apply various methods and techniques to your primary objective of recognizing his needs. The problem involves communication, how to get through to people. The excellent book *Getting Through to People*, by Jesse S. Nirenberg, can serve as a valuable guide. The seasoned negotiator is ever on the alert for tip-offs on the mental processes of his opposer, for clues that will reveal his motivations. He listens carefully to what the opposer says and meticulously observes the way he acts. His mannerisms and gestures, his recurrent phrases and modes of expression, are all clues to his thinking and his desires—his hidden needs.

ASKING QUESTIONS

The usual way to get information, of course, is to ask a question. Questions are windows to the mind. In an appropriate situation I have often asked my opponent, "What do you want from this negotiation? What do you expect? What would you like to accomplish?" Through such straightforward probes, in addition to other information, I often succeed in finding out my opponent's needs; what he is after, and then guide my future negotiating accordingly.

The proper use of questions in a negotiation as a means of recognizing needs generally involves three decisions: *what* questions to ask, *how* to phrase them, and *when* to ask them. The effect on the opposition is also an important consideration. The importance of properly phrasing a question is well illustrated by the following story. A clergyman asked his superior, "May I smoke while praying?" Permission to smoke was emphatically denied. Another clergyman, approaching the same superior, asked him, "May I pray while smoking?" To the question thus phrased, permission to smoke was granted.

It is equally important to know when to ask the question. Many a committee has been tied in knots and many a jury has been hung when the chairman or foreman started off the consideration with, "Let's find out where we stand before we begin the discussion," or "What do you think of this plan?" The timing of this question tends to freeze people into an immovable position.

Before asking people to take a position, it would be more advantageous to have everyone involved ask one or two questions. Postpone any commitment of position. Sincere questions requiring information should be sought. Leading questions suggesting an answer should be avoided. Questions should be used to make all participants familiar with available facts upon which to base their conclusions.

Under Anglo-Saxon jurisprudence, questions are used in both direct and cross-examination as a means of getting at the facts of a case. Until the Glorious Revolution of 1688, prisoners in treason and felony cases had no counsel, but even when counsel was finally allowed, the attorney was not permitted to address the jury, although he was allowed to cross-examine. Said Sir James Stephen: "Their cross-examination, therefore, tended to become a speech in the form of questions, and it has ever since retained this character to a greater or lesser extent."

As has been said, questions are used to uncover the needs of the opposition. As to the type of question to employ, it may prove useful to recognize that most questions fall into five categories:

1. General question: "What do you think?" "Why did you do it?" Question poses no limits, therefore the answers are uncontrollable.

2. Direct question: "Who can solve this problem?" Question contains limits, therefore answer is controllable within these limits.

3. Leading question: "Isn't it a fact?" (Answer controllable.)

4. Fact-finding question: "Where?" "Who?" "When?" "What?" (Answers controllable.) "How?" "Why?" (Answers sometimes controllable.)

5. Opinion-seeking question: "Is it?" "Do you think?" (Answers controllable.)

A lawyer in cross-examination tries to stay away from types of questions where the answers are uncontrollable.

The use of questions is a powerful negotiating tool and must be employed with discretion and judgment. The question determines the direction in which the conversation, argument, or testimony will move. The proper use of the question can often command an ensuing negotiation. The question you ask also controls the amount of information that is likely to be given back to you, much as turning the water faucet controls the flow of water. Questions stimulate the opponent to think, and often to start thinking critically about your proposition. By asking a specific question such as "What time is it?" or "Do you like watermelon?", we are demanding only a limited amount of specific information. Such questions are easy to answer, and in essence we are guiding or controlling the thinking of the other party. However, if we go to the other extreme and ask a general question such as "Why did you do it?" or "How did you do it?", then the answer is more difficult. Answering such questions forces your opponent to think a great deal more—with increasing risk that he will reexamine his premises or more critically reevaluate yours.

By the judicious use of questions you can easily secure immediate attention, maintain interest in the item under discussion, and direct the course that you want the conversation to take. Very often, by questions, the opposition can be led toward the conclusion you desire.

However, the use of questions raises several problems. One may innocently touch some emotional chord with a question and arouse considerable antagonism. I experienced this early when I asked a woman the simple question, "When were you born?" We were filling out a questionnaire and my query was perfectly routine; at least, so it seemed to me. But the woman was obsessed with the fear of growing old and the sense that life was slipping away from her. She reacted violently to what I considered a harmless question.

That woman taught me a lesson. I now proceed in this fashion: "On this Motor Vehicle form, they require a statement of your age. Some people prefer to state 'twenty-one' plus." Do you have any preference? Experience constantly shows that it is necessary to prepare the ground before asking questions.

Indeed, it is good practice to explain the reason for asking a question wherever this is feasible. It avoids trouble and embarrassment. Another way of avoiding unnecessary or unpleasant emotional response is to avoid asking forcing questions like "What is your excuse?" A nonforcing question, such as "How do you feel about the matter?", permits full and continuing discussion.

Preparing the ground before asking a question reminds me of the observation made by an architect friend. He was discussing communication, but his analogy applied to the asking of questions as well. Communication, he said, was like erecting a building. Preparatory information corresponds to the supplies for the building. If you sent the supplies to the site without plans having been previously furnished, the workmen might easily go ahead and put up any type of structure, not knowing what the architect had in mind. The correct procedure is for the architect to send the plans of the building to the job site first, and then, when the supplies arrive, the workmen will (we hope) put everything in its correct place, according to the plans. In questioning, you should give the other party a plan in advance of what you intend to gain from the conversation. If they have the plan first, then you can feed them the information, asking questions as you see fit. Ask questions and they will respond with much, if not all of the information, in a proper perspective.

A further problem in asking questions involves their form, which was touched on in the smoking story about the two clergymen. Do not ask questions that carry any vague implications, or that can easily be turned to your disadvantage. Tone of voice and wording should be given very careful consideration. This is important in the interest of clarity and in order to avoid any false inferences. Questions should be asked, not to score an advantage over your adversary, but for clarification. Well-conceived questions—concise and directed to the point under discussion—are a powerful negotiating tool for discovering the motives and recognizing the needs of the opposition.

Questions may also be used to control discussion in a negotiation. This is well illustrated in an article by Irving L. Lee in the *Harvard Business Review*, January-February 1954, entitled "Procedure for 'Coercing' Agreement." The problem involved the management group of a fairly large corporation, which seemed unable to formulate policies and reach meaningful decisions. It bogged down in basic disagreements between department heads. After much study the problem was solved by adopting a special procedure for the meeting. Mr. Lee's article explains:

The chairman was to proceed as usual until he sensed an impasse, *a situation in which conflict was well marked. This was likely to be any period when the talking seemed to accentuate differences, when there was evidence that the vote would be close, when the minority view was well stated, when people were contradicting each other. At this point he was to announce that the chair was raising a* Question *of Privilege for the Group and until further notice all talking which expressed any difference of opinion would be out of order. The chairman then would give the floor to any proponent of the view that aroused the controversy, who would be invited to state or restate the position without interruption. No counterstatement was to be permitted. The opposition's role was to be limited to the asking of questions. . . .*

The opposition may ask Questions for Clarification. *Questions of this variety are permitted: "What exactly is your procedure again . . . ?" "You said. . . ; did you mean this?" This process is supposed to forestall the impulse to disagreement until there is an effort at understanding. . . . It is also a way to to emphasize the belief that a proponent is entitled to every consideration in making his position clear, and that it will not be argued down before it is adequately stated. If listeners can be encouraged to wonder about what speakers mean, that may open rather than freeze the disputed position.*

The foregoing procedure works remarkably well. The use of the proper question technique steered the meetings into successful decisions and "coerced" the management group into agreements. Lee's article gives a marvelous insight into the use of questions for the purpose of guiding and influencing negotiations.

AFFIRMATIVE STATEMENTS

Skillful questioning can unearth a hidden assumption that is the basis of violent emotional reaction. Under such circumstances, it would be good strategy to make the simple statement, "I understand how you feel." This type of statement can remove the necessity for defiance because you are telling the opposer that he has been heard and understood, that you comprehend the validity of his point of view. Furthermore, telling him that you grasp his mental image may induce him to examine yours.

The proper use of statements is a way not only to control a negotiation but to present your opposer with the information you want him to have. Above all, try to maintain complete emotional control over any statement. Do not avoid emotional statements, but make sure that they advance—rather than stop—the negotiation. Machiavelli offers sound advice on how *not* to use statements: "I hold it to be a proof of great prudence for men to abstain from threats and insulting words toward anyone, for neither . . . diminishes the strength of the enemy; but the one makes him more cautious, and the other increases his hatred of you, and makes him more persevering in his efforts to injure you."

When a negotiation appears to be headed toward an impasse, it is good strategy to clear the air by a flat statement such as "It's the best we can do under the circumstances." This appeals to the opponent's need to know and understand, and forces him to reconsider the situation. You may decide that it is better strategy to take a less hard line or to compromise a point. In this event you might say, "I don't think we'll have much trouble with this point if we can get the other ne settled right." The statement shows a definite intention to make a concession on the first point, facilitating the progress of the negotiation. This is considered tacit communication and is a way of protecting one's position while at the same time indicating a possible adjustment. Another such illustrative statement is, "If you will lower your demand just a little, I'll do everything I can to sell it to my associates." However, if no concession or adjustment can be made, such statements will probably lead to a breakdown in the negotiation.

The proper use of statements demands close attention to the choice of words and phrases. Sometimes one word loaded with emotional significance can be disastrous. For example, one of the lawyers in a preliminary conference once used the adjectives "happy" and "rich" with unexpected results. He was trying to argue the benefits of a certain point that he claimed would make my client rich; somehow he also worked in the adjective "happy." In discussing the case later, my associate and I agreed that had the other lawyer used the comparative forms, "happier" and "richer," he would not have aroused our client's antagonism and stopped the negotiation. Even an important person who fancies himself as *happy* and *rich* does not mind being told, "This will make you *happier* and *richer*."

Here is an incident illustrating that by understanding the relative positions of the parties and using the proper words, one side can force the other to make the opening move.

J. P. Morgan once wanted to buy a large Minnesota ore tract from John D. Rockefeller. Rockefeller merely sent John D., Jr., around to talk.

"Well, what's your price?" Morgan asked.

"Mr. Morgan, I think there must be some mistake," John D., Jr., said. "I did not come here to sell. I understood you wished to buy." (You may recall that I stole a leaf from Mr. Rockefeller's book on behalf of my client in the old office building being demolished—Chapter II.)

Good technique involves much more than finding out your opposer's needs. The knowledge you have gained must be used in the most effective way. Webb and Morgan, in *Strategy in Handling People*, show how a master politician, Mark Hanna, exercised his skill in influencing a young businessman. It is an example of Need Theory in action.

The well-known politician, Mark Hanna, in 1896, when Mc-Kinley was running for President, organized the greatest Republican campaign in American history. He was attempting on a certain occasion to influence William Beer, a young New York business man. The response he wished was loyal Republicanism from Mr. Beer. He took advantage of the fact that the instinctive drives are always present in the organism, ready to be stimulated, and, since their responses are not fixed, may lead to various adjustments. The instinctive drives he stimulated were associated with family loyalty, a learned pattern involving more direct instinctive tendencies. The stimulus he used was a series of conversational remarks about Beer's father. He asked first, "Are you the son of Judge Beer in Ohio? You have an uncle down in Ashland, haven't you?" And so on about these great men, his relatives. Soon he had Beer talking and kept him discussing business for an hour or more. In this way he made a good friend of the younger man and held him for the Republican cause. He attached Republican adjustment to the parental and gregarious drives.

This interview between Mark Hanna and Mr. Beer should be regarded as a negotiation. Certainly Hanna had a definite goal—to persuade the young man to work for the Republican cause. The strategy Hanna employed appealed to the young man's need to belong, to be a part of his family group.

There are, of course, many ways of saying the blunt word which we all have to say—"no." The agent says, "Don't call us, we'll call you." In turning down an invitation to speak, a prominent man writes, "I am trying to keep down all outside activities to a barest minimum and it is on occasions when I have an invitation to do something as interesting as your proposal that I have to strengthen my character."

The unsold prospect says, "I'll think it over," or "I'll have to talk it over with my associates." The negotiator may say, "Let's lay that point aside for a moment—we'll come back to it later."

A Good Listener

Now consider the other means that can be employed—aside from asking questions and making statements—to recognize the needs of the opposition. One method is listening carefully to the words uttered by the opponent, his phrasing, his choice of expressions, his mannerisms of speech, his tone of voice. All give clues to the needs behind the statements he makes.

But if you would be a good listener, you must bear in mind that conversation or negotiation between individuals can proceed at various levels of meanings. Freud postulated that a dream can be interpreted on three different levels. Similarly, in many instances, a person's conversation or statement has several levels of meaning. For example, the opponent's statement on one level is the message that he *seems* to be trying to communicate. On a second level, it may be the message that we can infer from the way he speaks and the words he uses. On a third level, it may convey a meaning to us because it is linked with his manner of approach to the subject.

Listening is as much a persuasive technique as speaking. A successful listener must keep an open mind and strive to be free from bias and preconceived notions. Every statement can have at least two meanings. George Orwell, in 1984, gives certain slogans that, at first glance, would seem inconsistent. However, in agreement with Anatole Rapoport, we can see how, under certain circumstances and within certain limits, they make sense. Orwell's slogan, "Freedom is Slavery," can be true if there is no restriction on an individual's whims, because then the individual becomes the slave of his whims. His dictum, "War is Peace," makes some sense if we think of the unifying effects of war on the people of a nation: they are at peace with each other by being united in defense of their country.

Once you are ready to be a good listener, free from bias, anxious to learn something worthwhile about the needs of your opponent— what may you expect to hear?

Sandor S. Feldman, in his book *Mannerisms of Speech and Gestures in Everyday Life* (New York: International Universities Press, Inc., 1959), mentions many common mannerisms of speech which can be important in negotiation. Sometimes they may be attention-getting devices, sometimes they may mean the exact opposite of what the person appears to be saying. However, they give us some insight into the psychological factors present.

We frequently hear the expression, "By the way . . ." The speaker wants to give the impression that what he is about to say just entered his mind. But, nine times out of ten, what he says is very important and he is only pretending when he gives the casual introductory phrase. When a person begins his sentences with such words as "to be honest," "to tell the truth," "frankly," or "honestly," the chances are that he is *not* being frank or honest. Such expressions are used very frequently as a coverup.

"Before I forget" is really a nonsensical phrase. If a person is going to forget something, then he will never say it, it will be out of his mind. But if he hasn't forgotten and is going to say it, why introduce the matter with such a phrase? This expression is similar to "by the way," and in both cases there is a pretense that the matter that follows is unimportant. It is actually very important to the speaker and his fear of forgetting is untrue.

If a wife asks her husband, "Do you still love me?" and the husband answers, "Of course I do," the chances are that the wife will not be satisfied. The phrase "of course" is suspect. It has a shadow of doubt: it implies, "Sure, I love you, but not like in the old days." Had the husband answered with a simple "yes" it would have meant that he really loved her as always and his wife would have been contented. ("More than ever" would be an even better answer.) "Of course" indicates an absence of absolute assurance and the need for self-reassurance.

The term "naturally," so often used, is very similar to "of course" in meaning and implication.

The foregoing speech mannerisms are but a few of the more than 100 given by Dr. Feldman in his book. It should be understood that these phrases have psychological significance. They give us a clue to what is going on in the mind of the opponent. For this reason, listen attentively whenever your adversary makes a statement, and always be alert to spot hidden motives and needs revealed by seemingly innocent recurring phrases.

Sometimes you can become aware of a change in attitude on the part of the other person, not by *what* is said, but by *how* it is said. Assume that the negotiation has been going along smoothly, in a pleasant atmosphere, with all participants calling each other by their first names. Suddenly there is a switch to the surname, "Mr. Jones," or "Mr. Smith." This change is a sign of tension. Even worse, it may signal that an impasse has been reached.

NONVERBAL COMMUNICATION

Besides listening to your opponent in an attempt to learn his desires and needs, you must also closely observe his gestures. For example, in a friendly conference, if one member suddenly sits back and folds his arms with some abruptness, you would know at once that trouble had arrived. Gestures are tremendously important. They convey many shades of meaning, and have their psychological undertones and overtones. Therefore, observe the gestures of your opposer carefully and continuously to gain a clue to his thinking.

We are using the term "gesture" in the broadest possible sense. It includes much more than simple body motions. Tension can be shown by any number of signs such as blushing, contraction of the facial muscles, fidgeting, undue preoccupation, strained laughter or giggling, or even just staring in silence. Actually these are nonverbal means of communication. Dr. Sandor Feldman analyzes over fifty different gestures and other nonverbal expressions. These include bodily movement, posture, facial expression, and mannerisms of all kinds.

In any negotiation you are, of course, talking with your opposer. At the same time you are looking at him and seeing him. Psychologists make a distinction between *looking* and *seeing*. When we examine our outside world, we *look*. It is a form of spying and is objective. But when we *see*, we take in, we absorb, we comprehend the general impression subjectively. Suppose you meet a beautiful lady wearing a low-cut dress that displays the charm of her body. She wants you to *see* her and she will feel hurt if you do not register admiration in some form. But if you give her a look that's a stare and show that you particularly notice the low cut of her dress, then you are spying on her, you have offended her and she will feel compelled to withdraw. You are no gentleman.

Coughing frequently can have many implications. In some instances it has proved to be a form of nervousness, something the speaker depends on to help him go on talking. Often it is used to cover up a lie, or it serves to express doubt or surprise on the part of the listener if someone talks about himself with too much confidence or conceit.

Facial expressions are obvious means of nonverbal communication. But the "poker face" confronts us with a total *lack* of expression, a blank look. This very lack of expression tells us that a man does not want us to know anything about his feelings. In spite of the assumed mask, we can read his intent.

Blinking is a protective reflex action to keep the eyes moist and to remove accumulated dust particles. However, studies have shown that the rate of blinking is higher when we are angry or excited. Normal blinking is hardly noticeable, but when it becomes a mannerism it attracts our attention by its frequency and rapidity. In this abnormal state, blinking has been found to be connected with feelings of guilt and fear. It is used to hide something, and some research indicates that excessive blinking can serve as a lie detector.

Gestures, of course, can be used consciously and effectively in place of words, especially if the words themselves might not be tolerated or allowed. For instance, a lawyer may want to show his disagreement with the judge before a jury, or a soldier may want to indicate a difference of opinion with his top sergeant. But sometimes gestures are *too* expressive. They may reveal more than you want them to. The police claim they can always pick out the top man at a Mafia gathering by observing the extreme deference the others show him.

The skilled negotiator always keeps his eyes and ears fastened on his opponent. As Francis Bacon says in his essay *Of Cunning*, "It is a point of cunning, to wait upon him with whom you speak, with your eyes; as the Jesuits give it in precept: for there be many wise men that have secret hearts and transparent countenances." Emerson stated, "What you are speaks so loudly I cannot hear what you say."

However, no matter how closely you "wait upon him" with your eyes, you can not completely gauge the emotional state of your opponent. Nevertheless you must always be cognizant of the fact that emotions are lurking in the background whenever two or more people meet and talk. If you are dealing with an emotionally mature person, so much the better. Such a person can accept facts, even unpleasant ones, as concrete situations, to be handled as a means toward a solution of problems, rather than to be hated and thrust aside. It is the emotionally immature person who chooses techniques of negotiation for sheer emotional satisfaction, rather than for achieving a settlement.

The factors that affect emotions may be intangible. The room and setting in which a conference is held can have an effect on the emotions of the conference. The English political leader Ernest Bevin stated, from the experience of a lifetime spent in conferences, that he found that the ones held in cheerful, bright-colored rooms were more successful. The arrangement, location, and details of decoration can have an important influence on negotiation.

Aside from the surroundings, you can learn something by observing the way people move about in the conference room. If a person is interested in what is going on at the conference table, he will lean forward and become part of the group. The moment that he loses interest, he will withdraw or back away from the table.

Silent actions, gestures, and movements of all kinds have something to tell if you can read them correctly. In a situation where you want people to look to you as a person of authority, try to sit at the head of the table. Another seating arrangement involves two groups negotiating at a conference table. Try to sit on the side of the table with the opposing group. Then attempt to take issue with certain propositions proposed by your group, siding with the opposition. In minor things this appears to work, because the opposition begins to consider you as a member of their team. Thereafter they will listen most agreeably to your proposals for solving the points of disagreement.

The difficulty in evaluating nonverbal forms of communication is that they are connected, to a great degree, with the subconscious as well as the emotions. In coping with this, use your intuition (which I would define as a half-conscious blend of innumerable minute observations). Men defer to "a woman's intuition." And, while woman's intuition might be nothing more than man's transparency, women do, at least, seem more intuitive. A woman looks for the small details and observes them more accurately. Also, any woman who has brought up a child has had to communicate with the infant for two years on a nonverbal basis; this contact with the child from birth further develops intuition in women. We would all be better negotiators if we could acquire the skill in understanding gestures, the ability to observe details, and the intuition that seem to be innate in women.

However, to avoid any generalizations, let me relate this story. A jury was being picked in a criminal trial. As they started the selection, a prospective woman juror rose and told the judge that she wished to be excused. When she was asked why, she stated that one look at the accused had convinced her that he was guilty. With this the judge asked her to sit down and be quiet. The person she was pointing to was the district attorney.

Inborn gestures are very much the same in all parts of the world, but acquired gestures vary in different societies. In the United States, a man usually stands eighteen to twenty inches away when conversing face to face with another man. If talking to a woman, he will back off an additional four inches. But in Latin America men feel comfortable at thirteen inches. This is also true in France. Therefore, an American woman, let us say, in Paris, would feel imposed upon talking to a Frenchman at a distance of only thirteen inches, and he would feel most rejected were she to back away to twenty-four inches. (Could this be a reason why many women believe that Frenchmen are naturally aggressive?)

Cultural differences affect not only our use and interpretations of gestures but also our ways of thinking, and our attitudes toward the social structure. We have different ways of saying things. In English, the clock "runs"; but in Spanish, "el relojanda," he walks. In Spanish, a worker does not miss the bus; the bus left him. According to Stuart Chase, one conflict between the Indians and the early American settlers was due to a difference in the definition of property rights. To the Indian, no individual had exclusive "rights" in fishing or hunting lands. When the Indians sold land for a few knives or beads, they thought they were transferring additional hunting rights only. Naturally, when the palefaces exercised exclusive ownership over the lands, the Indians were bewildered and angry. The Europeans, on the other hand, regarded the Indians as cheats and liars who were not living up to their signed agreements. It was all due to different cultural concepts causing a breakdown in communication.

A cultural difference in the use of the word "no" causes endless trouble between Japanese and American businessmen. The Japanese businessman feels that if he answers with a complete negative he would cause the Americans to lose face. The American businessman, unaware of this, is often forced to negotiate without getting what he would feel is a clear response. Again, this is a breakdown in communication connected with cultural differences.

If you pump a German's hand more than once you confuse him. In India the color of a gift is quite significant: certain shades of green, for example, may give offense to the recipient. In the United States it is the custom for neighbors tò call on a new arrival, but in France it is just the reverse. The new resident is obliged to call on the old ones.

Nor are habitual gestures merely a matter of ethnic difference. A man puts on a coat, right arm first—a woman puts on the left arm first. When a man helps a woman to put on her coat, there is often, a slight awkwardness.

The point is this. To the negotiator, as the old song has it, "every little movement has a meaning all its own." The slight raise of the eyebrow, the tilt of the head, the sudden movement of the hand—all this is a language that the man who deals with people must understand.

It would seem, then, that successful negotiation demands smooth and unobstructed communication at all times. However, do not confuse communication with understanding. In more optimistic times it was believed that if people "understood" each other, there would be fewer breakdowns in communications. We do not have to "understand" people to communicate. Understanding and empathy are long-term goals. But in our time it almost seems that failure to communicate occurs *because* the parties feel they understand each other too well. As in the distinction between looking and seeing, understanding is the nervous (subjective) response to our communication (objective) attempts. I would, however, agree with Dostoevsky, in *The Brothers Karamazov*. "If people around you are spiteful, callous, and will not hear you, fall down before them and beg for their forgiveness; for in truth you are to blame for their not wanting to hear you." This failure in the communication chain is in oneself.

We must negotiate so that our opponent will reveal himself to us. We seek to recognize his needs, his motives, and his desires. We accomplish this by asking questions, by noting his mannerisms and context of speech, by observing his telltale gestures, and other nonverbal communication, by allowing for emotional stresses and cultural differences.

JONES ANALYZES PARKER

Let us return to Mantee, Inc., where Fred Jones, the vice-president for engineering and design, is *analyzing the needs* of his opposite number in the coming negotiations—the sales vice-president,

Lee Parker.

Of course Jones doesn't put it to himself that way. He asks himself, "What does Parker want out of all this, anyway?"

He asked Parker directly, and the answer turned out to be the obvious one: "All I want is to build sales volume by telling customers that the new '500' can be run at a greater speed than your department thinks feasible." But when Jones looks behind that obvious answer—when he looks at Parker the *man*—he comes up with a number of other needs.

For one thing, Parker wants to keep his job (safety need). And he wants to move up in the organization (esteem need). In this respect Parker is like most other people, including Jones himself. Nevertheless, these are needs which it will be useful to keep in mind.

Parker, like most men in the sales area, likes to be with people. And he likes people to like him. Jones must admit that Parker has made a number of overtures—lunch and so forth—in order to achieve a more friendly footing with Jones and his staff members. His actions have coincided with his words.

Along with this, Parker is proud of his ability and his professional standing. His office wall displays certificates and testimonials. He has always reacted with pleasure to any recognition that the company or outside organizations have accorded him. And his name has figured prominently in various newspaper releases. (Jones remembers with amusement how upset Parker was when the company paper spelled his name Lee Packer.)

Does this complete the list of Parker's needs? Upon further thought, Jones concludes that it does not.

While Parker is a gregarious man—with no small liking for recognition—he is not just a phony backslapper. Parker possesses an inner drive to do a good sales management job. He is, as they say, a self-starter. Any conclusion to the negotiation must take this self-respect into account.

In addition to trying to cultivate Jones and his associates, Parker has always tried to find out as much as he could about the way they operate. He is curious and inquisitive, particularly in areas that may affect sales performance or give him an edge in the corporate struggle. He prizes knowledge, respects differences of opinions, knows how to ask the right questions—and listens to the answers.

Finally, like most professionals, Parker likes the feeling of a "job well done." He likes things to be wrapped up neatly—no ragged edges. His office may be showy—but it is never untidy. With all his geniality, he runs a reasonably "taut ship" in the sales department.

With this understanding of Parker's needs, Jones feels that he is equipped to mount a strategy that will work.

IX

NEGOTIATING TECHNIQUES

When we have thoroughly prepared—when we have probed the assumptions existing on all sides—and, most particularly, when we have translated our knowledge into an understanding of *needs*, then we have mastered the "pieces" in negotiation.

How we deploy them· on the board is a matter of technique—strategy and tactics.

Those two words—strategy and tactics—are clearly differentiated in definition. In practice, however, it is often hard to tell whether a particular move is a bit of strategy or a tactic. In fact, the word "strategem" seems to combine the idea of strategy and tactic.

So in this chapter we will consider *strategy* as comprising the techniques used in the actual process of negotiation and *tactics* as devices used to implement the strategy.

Many of life's situations may be likened to the techniques we use when we dance in a crowded ballroom. When we move, where we go, how fast we go—all are determined by certain definite conditions: the tempo of the dance music, the partner, the other couples, our mental state, the presumed mental state of the other people, subconscious adherence to traffic rules and regulations, and so on.

Our strategy, for example, may be to circle the outside of the floor or it may be to penetrate to the center. The tactics we use—a particular step or change of direction—are governed by that strategy and also by the conditions around us at that moment.

The strategies set forth here are all designed to implement the Need Theory, which we have discussed at some length.

In studying the techniques of successful negotiation, we may think of them as so many tools which we learn to use. The Encyclopaedia Britannica defines a tool as "an implement or appliance used by a worker in the treatment of the substances used in his handicraft, whether in the preliminary operations of setting out and measuring the materials, in reducing his work to the required form by cutting or otherwise, in gauging it and testing its accuracy, or in duly securing it while thus being treated."

In this definition the phrases "preliminary operations" and "setting out and measuring the materials" are analogous to what we do in entering upon a negotiation. Our "preliminary operations" include research, consideration of needs and assumptions, and past experiences in the area under survey. We seek to gauge or measure in advance the hopes and goals of our adversary and ourselves, and their relationship to the conflict and frustrations of the problem being negotiated. During the course of the negotiation we employ other "tools" to accomplish our aims.

The inexperienced negotiator's strategy will be limited to a few simple and obvious devices. The expert negotiator, however, will employ a variety of means to accomplish his objectives. These means will involve "when" strategy or "how and where" strategy. They may involve the use of an agent as well.

"When" strategy essentially involves a proper sense of timing. It is easier to use in a negotiation when a new element enters the picture rather than where all elements are static. But properly applied, it can change a static situation into a dynamic one. "How and where" strategy involves the method of application and the area of application. Often it is advantageous to use two or more strategic approaches in the same negotiation. The more familiar you become with various strategic techniques, the better the chance of success in negotiating. Above all, do not rely on the behavior described in "Empedocles on Etna" by Matthew Arnold:

> *We do not what we ought;*
> *What we ought not, we do;*
> *And lean upon the thought*
> *That chance will bring us through.*

The following are examples of an overall strategy called "lowballing." This overall strategy combines apparent withdrawal and reversal, two of the basic strategies which will be fully discussed later in the chapter. It is applied on three levels: interpersonal, interorganizational (corporate), and international.

Selling automobiles is a highly competitive business. Many potential buyers try to take advantage of this by going from dealer to dealer with the request, "Just give me the price." Sooner or later the buyer will be hit with a "low-ball" price, one that is too low to be realistic and may even be below the dealer's cost. After the buyer has completed his appointed rounds, he will return to the low-ball dealer. He will expect that since he has completed his negotiation, there is nothing more to talk about. But the negotiations have just begun. The salesman will assail him with "extras" and high-priced financing. He may take the order and never deliver or switch to another car. The low-ball price will be blown to bits.

On the corporate level, the roles can be reversed. This time the seller is the victim, but the strategy is essentially the same. It is used when a business is in dire straits and must be sold immediately. The potential buyer offers a price or a deal that he knows is unrealistically good. He stalls but continues to offer the lure until all other potential buyers have lost interest. Then he offers his real price on a take-it-or-leave-it basis that the seller must accept.

On the international level, "dumping" of surplus goods is an "honest" form of low-balling. The selling price is low, so low that it drives the competing industries in another nation out of business. Then the rival nation enjoys a monopoly position and charges monopoly prices.

"When" Strategy

"When" strategy can be separated into several of the following: *forbearance, surprise, fait accompli, bland withdrawal, apparent*

withdrawal, reversal, limits, and *feinting.* Here are a few examples
of these types of strategy.

Forbearance ("waiting in haste"). Age is a great teacher of this
strategy. It is seldom used by the young or the ˙ insecure. Circumstances that warrant this strategy usually have elements that would
ordinarily tempt or provoke one to anger and impetuous action.
However, forbearance, or the withholding of such action, will be
used when it offers a greater reward. The reverse of forbearance is
the "rash act." Your judgment and values determine whether forbearance or acting immediately would be warranted.

The Quakers furnish an example. When members of a Quaker
meeting find themselves divided on a question, it is customary to
declare a period of silence. If the division still persists, the clerk
postpones the question for another time or a later meeting. This
can go on indefinitely until the question is resolved. Forbearance
thus avoids a direct conflict and eventually achieves a settlement.

Franklin D. Roosevelt used to tell a story about the Chinese use
of forbearance, based on four thousand years of civilization. Two
coolies were arguing heatedly in the midst of a crowd. A stranger
expressed surprise that no blows were being struck. His Chinese
friend explained, "The man who strikes first admits that his ideas
have given out."

Knowing when to stop is another element of forbearance. The
salesman must know when to stop talking. The attorney must know
when he has sufficiently cross-examined the witness. Earlier in this
book we related the story of the last tenant in the old office building. This negotiation was probably carried past the point where it
would have been wise to stop. Benjamin Disraeli recognized this
factor when he said, "Next to knowing when to seize an advantage,
the most important thing in life is to know when to forego an
advantage."

Surprise. This strategy involves a sudden shift in method, argument, or approach. The change usually is drastic and dramatic, although it need not always be so. Sometimes, in fact, the change can
be ushered in by as insignificant a sign as the alteration of the tone
of voice during a negotiation. Where you have carried on the entire
negotiation in a calm, even voice, one blowup can effectively make
the point. Winston Churchill illustrates this when he states: "I
have often tried to set down the strategic truths I have compre-
hended in the form of simple anecdotes, and they rank this way in

my mind. One of them is the celebrated tale of the man who gave powder to the bear. He mixed the powder with the greatest care, making sure that not only the ingredients but the proportions were absolutely correct. He rolled it up in a large paper spill, and was about to blow it down the bear's throat, but the bear blew first."

Fait accompli ("Now what can you do?"). This is a risky strategy but it is often a temptation to use it. It demands that you act, achieve your goal against the opposition, and then see what the other side will do about it. Those who employ this strategy must make an appraisal of the consequences in case it should prove to be a failure. An illustration of the unsuccessful application of this strategy was the attack by England, France, and Israel upon Egypt during the Suez crisis. They acted without prior consultation with the United States and hoped to present the world with a *fait accompli*. The United States intervened, however, and forced them to abandon the attack and to withdraw.

Bland withdrawal ("Who, me?"). An example of this strategy is the person who is caught red-handed but who turns and says, "Who, me?" The following illustration, while not directly related to negotiation, is in essence similar to maneuvers that are frequently encountered at the bargaining table. During the 1964 Presidential campaign, the press would attack Senator Goldwater for some statement he was alleged to have made. But Goldwater would say that he had been misquoted, or that he never had said anything of the kind, or that what he was accused of saying had been taken out of context, which altered the meaning altogether. However, the very frequency of his use of this strategy made it ineffective to all but his most ardent admirers. The newspapers just couldn't be wrong *all* the time—or so a majority of the voters thought.

A more successful approach is recorded in Boswell's *Life of Samuel Johnson:* A lady once asked him how his dictionary had come to define the word "pastern" incorrectly as the knee of a horse. Instead of making an elaborate defense, Johnson at once answered, "Ignorance, Madam, pure ignorance." By refusing to defend an obvious error, he disarmed his opponent and preserved the reputation of his dictionary as a whole.

Apparent withdrawal ("the man who wasn't there"). This strategy is made up of a mixture of forbearance, self-discipline, and a little deception. The aim is to convince your opponent that you have withdrawn, but without his knowing it, you are still in con-

...he situation. I used this strategy with a certain degree of ...... .n litigation involving the Rent Commission of the City of New York. The Rent Commission had determined that a hearing be scheduled at a time that was arbitrary and would prove detrimental to my client. The New York Supreme Court agreed that the scheduling of the proposed hearing would be detrimental. However, instead of granting an injunction, which had been requested, the Court merely suggested to the Rent Commission that it should postpone the hearing. In spite of the request of the Court, the Rent Commission went ahead with the hearing. I attended this hearing, but before it began, I had the official stenographer take down a statement for the record: "I warn everyone in attendance that this hearing is being held against the wishes of the Supreme Court; I will see to it that the Court is so informed and I will follow this matter through to its normal consequences. Moreover, I will not be a party to this hearing at this time." Having made this statement, I stalked out of the room. My withdrawal apparently was complete. However, unknown to the hearing officer of the Rent Commission, an associate of mine remained in the hearing room. Seated with a group of witnesses that had been called, he was prepared to take over in the event that the Rent Commission chose to go ahead with the hearing. This strategy, fortunately, was effective. The person in charge of the hearing was unsure of how to proceed. He called the Rent Commissioner for advice and was told to adjourn the hearing. Thereafter the Commissioner was persuaded that landlords are members of the community, and important ones, and that no one can be victimized without harm to everybody.

Reversal ("You can go forward, backward"). In this strategy, you act in opposition to what may be considered to be the popular trend or goal. Bernard Baruch once said that people who make money in the stock market are those who are the first in and the first out. By this he meant that you should buy when everyone was pessimistic and sell when the prevailing atmosphere was optimistic. This strategy may sound easy to execute, but in reality it is exceedingly difficult. Were it not so, we could all immediately become rich and powerful.

Gertrude Stein reversed a popular concept about Wall Street when she said that the money remains the same, it is merely the pockets that change.

New methods of communication have caused a reverse in many

traditional negotiating roles. I once had occasion to accompany a coffee purchaser on a buying trip into the Amazon jungle. I asked if he had any special method of negotiating for the coffee. He laughed and said: "I no longer negotiate. I am told how much I have to pay." He explained, "The most remote tribes in the Amazon that gather coffee have shortwave radios. They get the latest prices from the New York Coffee Exchange. They then add the cost of transportation, allow a small handling charge, and tell the buyer which price he must pay."

In the days following World War II the left-wing American Labor Party was prominent in New York politics. The ALP had formed an extreme aversion to a certain Brooklyn state senator, and had decided to "go after" him. They entered a candidate in the Democratic primary in his district, and there was a possibility that they might not only beat him, but gain control of the Democratic party in that district.

The senator refused to knuckle under and accept the endorsement of the American Labor Party. His problem was to prevent the ALP from "making an example" of him.

The senator and his staff decided on a strategy of reversal. They would make a bid to take over the American Labor Party in that district by entering a candidate in *their* primary. Squads of workers went out, and in two days enough signatures were accumulated to make an ALP primary fight feasible. Then the truce flag went up. The American Labor Party agreed not to fight the state senator if he would withdraw from their primary. The strategy worked perfectly.

Limits ("This is the absolute end"). The French have become famous for using the time limit as a strategic method. Restricted agenda is also a form of limit; that is, you will not negotiate on more than one subject or you will negotiate only in one particular manner. Restrictions on communication are also a use of this strategy; you will deal only through your agent, or you restrict the communication coming out of a negotiation.

When this approach is carried to an extreme, we have what is known as the "silent barter." Some tribes in Central Africa engage in a unique form of negotiation. The tribe desiring an exchange leaves its goods on the bank of a river. A neighboring tribe takes these goods, leaving other goods which they consider of equal value. If the first tribe is not satisfied, they leave the pile there until it is added to. In the event that no additions are made, the first tribe doesn't show up to do business again.

Feinting ("Look to the right, go to the left"). This involves an apparent move in one direction to divert attention from the real goal or object. It can also involve a situation in which you give your opponent a false impression that you have more information or knowledge than you really possess. This strategy has been successfully used in criminal trials. The district attorney is duty bound to tell the court all of the information and facts that he has in his possession. He may not withhold from the court any evidence that may be pertinent to the case, even though it may not help the prosecution. He does not always do this. Feinting strategy by defense counsel may lead the district attorney to believe that counsel is in possession of "all" the information and, therefore, the district attorney may feel the obligation *now* to tell the court all rather than continue to withhold pertinent facts.

Today, because of the speed of communication, a prepared governmental decision can be tested by feinting. The decision is released by "a reliable source" as a trial balloon before it is actually made. This gives the government an opportunity to test the different responses that might occur when and if such a decision is actually made. Then if opposition develops, it can either develop a strategy to counteract adverse responses or decide upon a new solution to the problem.

"How and Where" Strategy

Some of the principal forms of "how and where" strategy are *participation, association, disassociation, crossroads, blanket, randomizing, random sample, salami, bracketing.*

Participation ("We are friends"). In this form of strategy you strive to enlist the aid of other parties in your behalf, to act either directly or indirectly. International alliances like NATO or the Warsaw Pact are good examples of this form. Each participant will probably assist the other with his individually different strategy. This includes "me too," strategy, such as has been used in the maritime labor relations field. As reported in the *New York Times*, August 28, 1965: "Almost every [Maritime] Union has a clause in its contract that if something better than what the contract terms delineate is later granted to another union, it will be automatically added to the first contract." The *Times* stated that "this is one of the chief reasons why the Merchant Marine strike went through its 73rd day without a settlement." It would appear that this strategy of the union backfired.

Association. This technique is used extensively in the advertising field. Testimonials assert that a famous person uses and endorses a certain cigarette, soap, hairdressing, or some other product. These testimonials associate the product with the rich, important, powerful personages who endorse it. Many people identify themselves with these personalities and begin to use the product.

Many businessmen who feel that they would be too sophisticated to be influenced by this advertising tactic fail to realize it is related to the business device of electing famous military, scientific, or political figures to the board of directors of corporations. The corporation is now supposed to benefit from the "halo" effect of these famous people.

Disassociation ("Who is your friend?"). Obviously this strategy is the reverse of association. A product, or more frequently a cause, is discredited by showing that unsavory characters are connected with it. This is a form of strategy that is often used in politics by both the extreme Left and the extreme Right. It calls the attention of the general public to the kind of people who are associated with a particular movement, cause, or proposal. It is hoped that the assumed reputation of the people connected with the movement will steer the public in the opposite direction, away from the association.

Crossroads ("intersect, entwine, and entangle"). In this form of strategy you may introduce several matters into the discussion so that you can make concessions on one and gain on the other. Minor issues, however, should be handled carefully. If you take too much time with them, the other side will start fighting back as if they were large issues. Then as the opponent gives in, he does it expecting a concession on a major issue. It also covers the situation where you bring forces, arguments, or pressures of some kind to bear on a particular object of the negotiation. This corresponds to a military tactic in which machine guns are placed so as to create a devastating cross fire and cover an area more thoroughly. In chess, this approach is used where pressure from many pieces is applied to one of the opponent's pieces or spaces.

Blanket ("shotgun"). The aim of this strategy is to cover as large a field as possible. It is well illustrated by the story of a young man who, whenever he went to the movies, picked out a seat next to a young lady. He would then suggest that she kiss him. His friend, on hearing this, said to him, "I imagine that you get your face slapped quite a few times." The young man replied, "Yes, I do, but I also get an awful lot of good kissing."

There is a certain group of businessmen who are called "deal men." They are in a sense business brokers, trying to bring together the buyer and seller or other elements required. Different techniques are used by the more sagacious. However, the ordinary deal man uses the "shotgun" method. Without regard to the consequences, he brings together as many people as possible, hoping that two of them may match up and permit him to make a commission. I myself prefer the "rifle" method.

Randomizing ("outbluffing by chance"). In this strategy, you make use of the law of chance to defeat the "bluffing advantage" in a game. For example, I had become quite proficient in the game of "guessing which hand the coin is in." By sleight of hand I fooled my son over and over again. He continually made a very high percentage of wrong guesses. Then he decided to base his guesses on the law of chance. He tossed his own coin to decide his choice. When he did this he guessed right at least 50 per cent of the times, over a long period of guesses and tosses. Randomizing, using the law of chance, improved his score by making my bluffing useless.

There will always be those fortunate people—the clappers in the bell-shaped curve—who can deal with statistics and the laws of probability to ring the bell. One such person was Baron Long, a famous gambler in the 1920's. Baron Long made his big killing at the Agua Caliente race track in Mexico. He used the maneuver of "building."

"Building" calls for a system of betting in which off-track bookmakers pay at track odds. The track odds are, of course, based on the total amount wagered at the track on each horse. When the off-track bookies pay at track odds they are able to keep for themselves the percentage taken off by the track for expenses and taxes.

To make his killing Baron Long had to rig the track odds so that the payoff on the fastest horses—the favorites—was far greater than the risk involved. To do this he had a large group of associates line up at the track betting windows. They kept the public from betting the favorites. At the same time they were upsetting the odds by wagering on the poorer horses in the race.

Meanwhile, other associates were making huge bets on the favorites with the off-track bookies. The favorite won, at track odds approaching 1,000 to 1. The bookies who did not go out of business were forced to pay off at that price.

After this the bookies changed their strategy to prevent a recurrence of this maneuver. Nevertheless, the same trick was worked in Great Britain in 1964 at a greyhound track. The mastermind, a gambler named John Turner, lined up his men in front of the windows, *à la* Baron Long. They manipulated the odds on the race so that the payoff on the winning combination was 9,875 to 1. The bookmakers, who operate legally in Great Britain, went to court—but in 1965 a high court judge found nothing illegal in the strategem. The judge described it as a battle of wits in which Mr. Turner had come out on top. Obviously even bookies who do not learn from the past are doomed to repeat it.

There was once a particular type of con man known as the "Murphy man." The Murphy man used the strategy of randomizing. In the 1920's, the name and game originated in the area west of Times Square known as Hell's Kitchen. This section was heavily populated by Irish immigrants. The technique of the con man was to approach a stranger in the area, offering, for a price, to obtain a girl for him. If the victim gave him some money, the con man would then take him to a tenement house and instruct him to "ring Mrs. Murphy's doorbell," the odds being that there was a Murphy somewhere in the building. You will note today that this con game is still in existence. The names may have changed but the game is the same.

Random sample ("fibbers can figure"). This involves picking a sample and assuming that the sample that has been chosen will represent the whole. Political parties use this quite frequently to show the general public that a survey they have taken indicates that their candidate will be the winner. The deception consists in planting the people who take the survey in carefully selected areas. Statistics presented in negotiations are often based on random samples and must be closely scrutinized. How to detect biased samples, deceptive averages, and other irregularities is set forth in *How to Lie with Statistics* by Darrell Huff and Irving Geis.

There is the story of the traveler who was reluctant to fly in an airplane because he heard about people carrying bombs on planes. Discussing his fear with a friend, a statistician, he asked him, "What is the probability of a bomb being on the same plane that I might take?" The statistician figured it out and came up with something like 1 in 10 million. The traveler thought a while, and then said, "What is the probability of two bombs being on the same plane?" The statistician worked it out and replied, "I wouldn't be concerned. The probability is so remote, it could never happen in your lifetime." A year later the traveler met the statistician and the statistician asked him how things were going. "Oh, I've been flying all over. Now I'm no longer concerned about someone bringing a bomb aboard the plane that I'm on. I always carry a bomb with me."

Difficult as it may be to believe, a story has it that the Beatles owe part of their early success to the strategy of random sample. The late Brian Epstein, their manager, recognized the group's potential long before the general public knew of their existence. The Beatles' initial popularity was limited to the Liverpool area. Their records did not show up on the overall hit charts.

Brian Epstein decided to change all of this. He sent his agents into the various towns in England where the record charts were compiled. Within a concentrated period of time they bought up Beatle records (which Epstein then resold in his own record shops). The Beatles' popularity rating zoomed—and they were off to the races. One result of this strategy is that Britain has been helped to balance its books for a year or two.

In the fall of 1967 when President Johnson's popularity was at a low ebb, certain backers arranged for polls to be taken. The polls were restricted to areas where Johnson was likely to be very strong. Furthermore, they pitted him against not too strong opponents. The results were then publicized as an upturn in the President's popularity. The research firms involved were chagrined, but the backers of the polls had accomplished what they had set out to do.

Salami ("degreewise"). This strategy involves taking something bit by bit, so that you eventually get possession of the entire piece. Mátyás Rákosi, General Secretary of the Hungarian Communist Party, is credited with having given this technique its name. Rákosi explained the "salami" operation to his collaborators as follows: "When you want to get hold of a salami which your opponents are strenuously defending, you must not grab at it. You must start carving for yourself a very thin slice. The owner of the salami will hardly notice it, or at least, he will not mind very much. The next day you will carve another slice, then still another. And so, little by little, the whole salami will pass into your possession." This nibbling process has been very much in evidence in the actions of the Communists since World War II.

In line with this approach, never make it appear that you are trying to take anything away from your adversary, no matter how slight. A good salesman in the nut store does not overload the tray with nuts and then remove a portion of them in order to get the proper weight. He gradually builds the order up to the proper weight, adding, never subtracting.

Bracketing ("how to make and hit the mark"). This expression is taken from the old artillery term in which the first shell was arranged to fire above the target, the second below the target, and thereafter this bracket was split successively until reduced to an on-target distance. An executive of a large business firm explained his ability to retain his top position by saying he used the strategy of bracketing. His duties require him to make many decisions. He does not spend all of the decision time trying to be "right on target." He is satisfied if he is in the right area. Thereafter he merely cuts down the degree of error.

AGENCY

The possible uses of an agent in negotiation are so important that they are being presented here as a separate strategic topic. It has been contended that partisan zeal should be every attorney's byword. It should also be the byword of every agent representing parties to a negotiation.

Sometimes it is expedient to let an agent conduct your negotiation for you. Certain circumstances may force you to such a decision; it can occur in any negotiation. Francis Bacon, in his essay *Of Negociating*, writes of agents:

It is generally better to deal . . . by the mediation of a third than by a man's self. . . . In choice of instruments, it is better to choose men of a plainer sort, that are like to do that that is committed to them, and to report back again faithfully the success, than those that are cunning to contrive out of other men's business somewhat to grace themselves, and will

*help the matter in report for satisfaction sake. Use also such
persons as affect the business wherein they are employed; for
that quickeneth much; and such as are fit for the matter; as
bold men for expostulation, fair-spoken men for persuasion,
crafty men for inquiry and observation, forward and absurd
men for business that doth not well bear out itself. Use also
such as have been lucky, and prevailed before in things
wherein you have employed them; for that breeds confidence,
and they will strive to maintain their prescription.*

Here is an instance in which the role of an agent was played
with good results.

A conference had been arranged between my client and his adversary. His attorney and I were also to be present. My client
failed to show up at the appointed time. After waiting for him
quite a while, I suggested that we begin the negotiation. As our
talk went on, I found that I was being singularly successful in getting the opposition to make commitments; but every time they
asked me for a commitment, I would say, "Well, I'm sorry, but I
only have limited authority." By serving in the role of an agent, I
secured many concessions for my client without committing him
in any way.

The technique of giving the negotiating agent only limited authority or tying him down to specific instructions beyond which he
dare not commit himself has proved extremely advantageous in
many cases. The opposing party, realizing that the agent is bound
to live up to his instructions, is more restrained in his demands.

In certain cases the agent may have an additional individual
incentive to secure a favorable settlement. For example, when an
insurance company represents a defendant in an automobile acci-
dent case, it is acting as an agent on behalf of the defendant. It
also has an incentive to get the best possible settlement because
it will have to pay for any damages awarded to the plaintiff, together with court costs.

Sometimes it is judicious to delegate all authority to an agent.
Businessmen do this when they place their employees under fidelity
bonds. Should any case of theft or dishonesty arise, they are re-
lieved of the task of prosecuting or condoning the crime. They do
not have the authority to act because they have placed or delegated
full authority in the hands of the insurance company. This ar-

rangement saves them from having to make many troublesome decisions. One man I know achieves almost the same degree of protection and avoids involvement as well—without the expense of bonding his employees. He requires every applicant for a job to fill out the regular bonding form, which he then simply files away without taking out a bond. The employee is under the impression that he has been bonded and is deterred from committing a dishonest act by the thought that he would then be up against the bonding company, which would be a lot harsher with him than the employer is likely to be.

Although an agent is often desirable in one's *own* cause, it also follows that in negotiations it is best to avoid dealing with the adversary's agent. If at all possible, deal with the principal. A corollary to this is, Never take for granted that you are actually dealing with the principal or even the proper party.

A pertinent case, which occurred some time ago, gives a bizarre illustration of the main point and its corollary. My client's father had vanished for approximately six months after the United States entered World War II. It was only by chance that a relative discovered that the father had been working as a cook for a construction firm that had a contract to do some defense installations in Iran. Since the father was an accomplished linguist, it seemed strange that he should take a job as a cook.

Some years later my client related the story to me and said that he had been trying unsuccessfully to collect the proceeds of an insurance policy provided for all employees of the construction firm. The attorney who had been handling the case for my client heard many different stories explaining the father's conduct. One that seemed most convincing was that the father was working for the OSS and was sent on a secret mission to Iran to ascertain what was going on along the Russian border. Having obtained the information, he wanted to get home quickly. Therefore, he started a fight with a superior. He was summarily discharged and was placed on a steamer sailing to the United States. Somewhere in the Atlantic, the steamer was torpedoed and sunk by a German submarine. There were a few survivors. From their written statements it was ascertained that the father was last seen floating on a raft. These circumstances, plus the passage of several years, were enough to establish the fact that he was dead. However, the construction firm for whom he worked told the attorney that they had discharged him prior to his death and therefore were no longer responsible. The lawyer pointed out that the man might have been a government agent. In answer the construction firm said that this was all the more reason for not paying any claim. Three years of threats, claims, and lawsuits were unproductive. This was the situation when I was introduced into the picture, being retained and substituted as attorney.

After an initial investigation, it was determined that the construction firm had worked in Iran under a cost-plus government contract. If the firm could be made to pay any money, they would be reimbursed by the federal government. Therefore, I determined that my approach would be to circumvent the construction firm and go directly to the government agency that had employed the firm. I presented my claim there.

The government agency to which the claim was made was receptive. Within one week after I had exhibited all the necessary documentation and evidence, the U.S. government paid the full claim. I never did find out if the man was or was not with the OSS. However, it is my firm belief that the father was indeed one of those heroic men who had sacrificed both their identities and their lives during World War II.

The lesson to be learned from this case is always to deal with the man who signs the checks.

International corporations now use bicultural people as a type of mediator or agent. Such companies are now familiar with the kinds of cultural conflicts they meet when they set up operations in a foreign country. For example, in India a local executive will tend to hire people exclusively from his particular area. Since employment is priceless to the Indian, this sort of regional nepotism is hard to combat. The local man is constantly beset by his employees—who are also his neighbors. They feed him the "inside story" about the "others."

Bicultural managers, who have been born in India but have lived abroad, are better able to cope with this situation. They have a broader perspective and can be trusted by all parties. Thus they interpret the conflicting parties to each other.

Life, in its capriciousness, can bestow the role of mediator on one who was previously uninvolved. During the great blackout of the eastern United States in 1965, young boys in midtown New York were permitted full authority over all traffic when they jumped into the snarled intersections and began to help out.

STRATEGY AT WORK

Now let's rejoin our friend Fred Jones, vice-president for engineering and design at Mantee, Inc. The time has come for Fred to sit down across the table from Lee Parker, the sales vice-president, and work out an answer to the problem of the "500." Jones and Parker are accompanied by aides—but they are the negotiating parties.

As we have seen, Fred Jones has done quite a bit of homework to get ready for the negotiation. He opens up with a restatement of his department's position.

"Lee, I've gone back over the memos that were exchanged before the '500' went on the market. It's all quite clear. We specified that the equipment was not to be run at more than 1,300 per hour. There's no doubt that this condition is not being observed, is there?"

"Fred," Parker replies, "I've gone over the pieces of paper too. I didn't have to—I remember it all very well. That was what you said —but that was some time ago. As I understand it, you fellows were continuing to work on the machine to improve it. You felt that in a reasonable period we could specify a much higher capacity."

"Sure," says Jones, "but we didn't say when that would be. And the time hasn't come yet. The fact of the matter is that the '500' cannot be guaranteed to stand up in service at more than 1,300 units. And your people are encouraging customers to run it too fast."

"Oh, we're not encouraging them, Fred. We don't offer a guarantee. Our men have instructions to tell the customer what the recommended output should be."

Jones leans back. "But you know as well as I do that, unless the thing is controlled, such a recommendation is not going to be made very strongly."

Parker frowns. "If you are implying that my salesmen misrepresent the '500,' you'd better have proof."

Now it happens that Jones *has* some pretty good proof which he could produce at this time. Instead he takes another tack.

"Don't you think it's dangerous to sell equipment that may well break down in operation? Won't that hurt our reputation—and our sales?"

"Look," Parker replies. "We're most concerned about the company's reputation. But we can't control what customers do after they have the stuff. And, let's face it—you guys are always conservative about these things. Remember the battles we had over that other new line two years ago? The customers had to prove to us that it could handle a variety of jobs. Your department was the last to admit it. If the sales force hadn't pushed it, we'd still be kidding around with the project."

Jones can't deny that—nor does he intend to. "That doesn't prove anything about the '500.' "

"Well, Fred, maybe this does." Parker shoves a fat folder across the table. "Those are all letters from customers. They're all running the '500' at high speeds—and having no trouble at all. Look at them."

But Jones doesn't look. "All unsolicited testimonials?"

"What does 'unsolicited' mean? Sure, when this thing came up, our men went and checked with their customers on how the equipment was being used. But nobody twisted any arms."

"Any complaints in this file? Any letters from people who *have* had trouble with the equipment?"

"No."

Now Jones leans forward. "What would you say if I told you *we* had quite a few complaints from customers that show the equipment *can't* be operated at those speeds?"

Parker's eyes narrow. "I'd say you had gone behind the back of the sales department and loused up customer relations to get them. If you go out of your way to solicit complaints, that's what you're doing. *Do* you have letters like that?"

Jones shakes his head no. "But you'll admit we could have gotten them. And when you consider that—what's this file of yours worth? You just went out and collected the positives."

Now Parker chuckles disarmingly. "Fred, I figured you'd take care of the negatives. OK, these endorsements aren't worth too much. But let me show you something that *is* worth a great deal. Take a look at these sales figures and projections—not only for the '500' but for the whole line. This is the lifeblood of our business, Fred. You can't possibly want us to discontinue a campaign that is working this well. The company can't permit it, the stockholders won't permit it." Parker has played his hole card. It looks like an ace.

But Jones is ready to play *his* hole card. This is the result of all his preparation. He is ready to propose a solution in which each side can emerge a winner.

Jones says, "We don't want to ask you to discontinue a campaign which is working well. But of course you fellows are not just looking for the quick buck. You're as concerned as we are about the long-term needs of our customers and of Mantee."

Parker nods. "Sure we are."

"Both of us are trying to contribute to that in our different ways. We develop products. You sell them. If we can cooperate with one another, we each do a better job."

Parker looks cautious. "If cooperating with you means we sell with one hand tied behind our back—I don't see how we can do that."

"It doesn't mean that at all. Now . . . here's what I propose, Lee. First of all, we will no longer insist that customers be limited to 1,300 units per minute on the '500.' Instead, we propose that you tell customers it's absolutely guaranteed for 1,300—but that we feel it's capable of a much higher rate."

Parker is listening carefully.

Jones continues. "Give your customers all the facts. And tell them that if they cooperate, we will give them certain price breaks. If they run the machine at high speeds—and agree to give us information about its performance—we will give them a discount. My department will undertake to make sure replacement equipment is quickly available to any customer in that category, so he won't be inconvenienced by a breakdown.

"Your salesmen can collect the information—and feed it back to my engineers. Working together, I don't doubt that we can— very quickly—improve the '500' even beyond what we had hoped. See how it works?"

Parker says, "Well, some of the details are cloudy, but I get the general picture."

Jones goes on. "The participating customer is able to get maximum value out of the '500'—with minimum risk. He gets a break in price. And there is another intangible benefit—he *knows* the company is taking his reactions into account in its research and development. Nothing wrong with that, is there?"

Parker warily shakes his head, no.

"What's in it for us in Design? The advantages are obvious. We protect the reputation of our product. At the same time we get fast, practical information from the firing line—and this is the lifeblood of our effort.

"And what are the advantages to you and your salesmen? You're able to continue to stress a product advantage. You can be completely frank with your customers—in a way that no competitor has ever been. Your men work closely with the customer, building up valuable relationships. You participate in the design and production functions, which are most important to you. And you contribute to an overall solution which will enhance our reputation throughout the industry. How does it sound to you, Lee?"

Parker sits quietly. "There's a hell of a lot there," he says. "Let's go through it again."

The meeting takes an hour more—but the solution is essentially the way Jones outlined it.

It is an example of the art of negotiation carried into practical action.

X
LIFE
ILLUSTRATIONS

In preceding chapters we have listed the different needs, the three levels of negotiations, and the six varieties of application. Here is a complete tabulation of these categories:

NEEDS

I.	Homeostatic Needs
II.	Safety and Security Needs
III.	Love and Belonging Needs
IV.	Esteem Needs
V.	Self-Actualization Needs
VI.	To Know and Understand Needs
VII.	Aesthetic Needs

NEGOTIATIONS, LEVELS OF APPROACH

Level A   Interpersonal

Level B   Interorganizational
Level C   International

VARIETIES OF APPLICATION

Variety 1   Negotiator works for the opposer's needs.
Variety 2   Negotiator lets the opposer work for his needs.
Variety 3   Negotiator works for the opposer's and his own needs.
Variety 4   Negotiator works against his needs.
Variety 5   Negotiator works against the opposer's needs.
Variety 6   Negotiator works against the opposer's and his own needs.

When we apply these in combination, we find that there are 126 possible gambits of negotiation, as reproduced in the chart on p. 131. This is only one method of combination. By further enlarging and defining the number of possibilities becomes infinite.

In this chapter we will consider each of the gambits—and give an example of each.

Use this chapter as a generator of ideas and as a reference guide. Although you may never find yourself in many of the situations presented, the examples may well suggest strategy and tactics for *other* situations. And in a number of cases you may find examples that bear directly on negotiations you have conducted, are conducting, or will conduct in the future.

You can utilize these applications from the point of view of negotiator and/or opposer. Because you may find yourself on either side in the following negotiation illustrations, I have used the word "opposer" to designate the opposite party rather than the word "opponent," which may carry an adverse connotation.

But let us not forget the underlying philosophy of negotiating success—everyone wins.

I. HOMEOSTATIC NEEDS

1. NEGOTIATOR WORKS FOR OPPOSER'S HOMEOSTATIC NEEDS

Interpersonal. The drama of a would-be suicide (the opposer) who is persuaded to preserve his own life is an example of an individual (the negotiator) working for another person's homeostatic need. The object of the negotiation is to save a human life, and the negotiator will run the gamut of techniques in an effort to

THE STRUCTURE AND ORDER OF GAMBITS
IN THE NEED THEORY OF NEGOTIATING

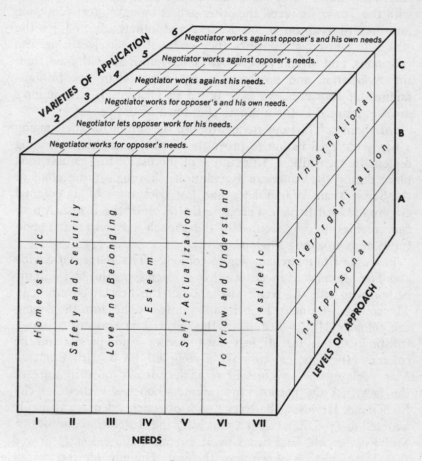

This matrix figure represents a block of 126 individual cubes, each of which stands for a different negotiating gambit.. These cubes can be further subdivided.

persuade the other person that his life is worth retaining.

Interorganizational. The periodic New York City newspaper strikes in the 1960's were an example of rivals working together. The members of the Publishers Association suspended publication of their newspapers when any member was struck. In 1965 the *New York Times* (the opposer) was struck, and six other daily newspapers (the negotiators) suspended publication. The *Times*, which carried more advertising than any of the others, was the chief economic rival of the other members. By closing shop along with the *Times*, however, the other papers brought great economic pressures to bear on union leaders and others affected by the strike. The financial pressures they endured themselves were also enormous, and several papers were later forced to withdraw from the Association and finally to merge rather than risk business failure. Of course, as we have noted in Chapter II, the union's excesses resulted in the ultimate shutdown of the papers.

International. Nations frequently use the gambit of encouraging a newly emerged nation to prove its viability and then extending diplomatic recognition. An example of the use of this gambit took place during the American Revolution. In 1763, at the close of the Seven Years War, France had lost back most of its colonial empire to Great Britain. Therefore the revolt of the British American colonies in 1775 seemed to the French a heaven-sent opportunity for weakening England.

Pierre de Beaumarchais, whose comedies *The Barber of Seville* and *The Marriage of Figaro* still live as operas, organized a dummy corporation with the secret assistance of the French government. The company funneled French money and supplies into the American colonies. However, France (the negotiator) was not being altruistic in all this. Her strategy was to keep a steady pressure on the colonies (the opposer) to make a complete break with England. Many colonists were reluctant to make such a move in spite of the fact that the patriot cause seemed hopeless without official French aid. However, the Declaration of Independence was finally adopted in 1776, more than a year after the Revolution had begun. Still France held back from overt aid until the colonists proved they had a chance of winning the war. Happily for the patriot cause, John Burgoyne, a boring playwright and a worse general, provided the opportunity in 1777, when he invaded New York from Canada. Led into a trap at Saratoga, Burgoyne and his army surrendered.

Proving that they were able to maintain themselves successfully, the colonists found the benefits enormous. Within a few months France, Spain, and the Netherlands recognized the United States.

Not only could the new nation obtain money and supplies from them, but the French Navy was a constant threat to the British Isles. The British Navy had to split its fleet: one part blockaded France while the rest was employed in America. The final victory at Yorktown was possible only because the French fleet was put at Washington's disposal. Washington's army pinned the British forces against the coast and the French fleet prevented their rescue by sea.

2. Negotiator Lets the Opposer Work for His Homeostatic Needs

Interpersonal. It is even possible to negotiate with a prisoner. Although his freedom of action is controlled and his area to negotiate limited, he can be made to work for his homeostatic needs. Nevertheless, some guards (the negotiators) apply additional pressures by threatening to put him (the opposer) on a diet of bread and water or in a "sweat box"; apparently his desire to break prison rules soon evaporates. The prisoner has been negotiated into a position of working for his basic need to survive.

Interorganizational. Some giant organizations (the negotiator) have used this gambit with success. The owner of a small gasoline station (the opposer) might operate with such a low overhead that he can afford to cut prices to increase his sales. A large company can prevent him from taking this action. Although the large company wants high gasoline prices in the long run, it can cut prices in the short run so drastically that the very existence of the small company is in jeopardy. The threat of such a price war is usually enough to cause the station operator to work to maintain his prices and keep himself in line. John D. Rockefeller and other business tycoons at the turn of the century understood this negotiating gambit all too well.

International. At the beginning of the twentieth century, 562 native states still existed within British India. These states based their independence on treaties their rulers had made with the British during the eighteenth and nineteenth centuries. Within their own domains the native princes ruled as absolute monarchs. Yet many of the states were small and most of the princes owed their thrones to the protection of the British Army. In their circumstances the princes (the opposers) were quite willing to work for their thrones, for their homeostatic need, by offering Britain (the negotiator) economic-support and military loyalty even at the expense of their own people.

3. NEGOTIATOR WORKS FOR THE OPPOSER'S AND HIS OWN HOMEOSTATIC NEEDS

Interpersonal. The extraordinary success of the fight against polio as opposed to other diseases is an example of this gambit. Franklin D. Roosevelt was crippled by the disease in 1921. When he became President twelve years later, he put his efforts into establishing the National Foundation for Infantile Paralysis. His appeals to the nation for funds met with great success, partly because of the openhandedness so typical of many Americans, but also because of the fear of this dread disease. Thus Roosevelt (the negotiator) worked to establish the Foundation for his own need and that of others (the opposers) to conquer polio and end the threat of physical impairment or even death.

Interorganizational. The 1961 conviction of twenty-nine major electrical manufacturers for price fixing brought to light a hitherto successful, albeit illegal, use of this negotiating gambit. It was to the advantage of the companies and officials involved to keep prices artificially high. To protect profits, the lifeblood of industry, they (negotiator and opposers) secretly agreed to fix prices on their products and to rig bids so that each company would receive its "fair" share of business.

International. National survival is a basic homeostatic need. In the nuclear age, nations at last have the power to annihilate their opponents in a single strike. Yet this awesome power has not and probably will not be put to use by either the United States or the Soviet Union. No treaty between the two nations guarantees that nuclear weapons will not be used. However, by tacit agreement both (negotiator and opposer) have accepted the deterrent power of nuclear weapons. If one nation should use them, it could expect swift and devastating retaliation. Sir Winston Churchill, in his last major speech as Prime Minister, summed up the grim reality of the situation: "It may well be that, by a process of sublime irony, we shall reach a stage in this story where safety will be the sturdy child of terror and survival the twin brother of annihilation."

4. Negotiator Works Against His Homeostatic Needs

Interpersonal. The variety of application may seem paradoxical, but there are many instances where this type of gambit had forced the issue and brought the negotiation to a successful conclusion. An article in the October 2, 1964, issue of the *New York Times* provides an example:

> A *special mission to Saigon last summer taught Herbert Schmertz how hazardous the life of a lawyer-labor arbitrator can be. Shortly after he checked out of his hotel, a bomb blew up on the floor where he had been staying. "I was sent by the government to study labor relations in the port of Saigon and found myself in a hotel whose staff was on strike,"* he explained. *"When one employee threatened to disembowel himself in the lobby, it was too much. I got out, and I just made it in time. The prefect of Saigon later settled the strike by threatening to arrest the hotel manager. It was efficient but it's not the way we mediate in America."*

The lawyer arbitrator was wrong. It *is* one of the ways Americans negotiate. However, he failed to see the structure into which these techniques fit. He failed to realize that the child who holds his breath to force his mother to give in to his desires, or the insane person who threatens to slash his wrists if the guard will not give him a cigarette, is using the identical method. In each case the individual (the negotiator) works against his physiological need to gain his objective. Undoubtedly these acts are considered by some to be irrational, but they are not. They are well-thought-out and effective means of achieving the desired goals. Only those who cannot rationalize the other person's premises for these acts consider them irrational.

Interorganizational. For a business organization (the negotiator) to deliberately work against its need to increase its income would also seem at first glance to be an irrational act. It would be much like the story of the merchant who does a land-office business by selling below cost. His explanation: "I may lose a little on each piece, but I make it up in the volume." Yet many large retail corporations (the negotiators) have found it to their advantage to sell loss leaders or bait merchandise. These are items sold at little or no profit to lure customers (the opposers) into the store. Their individual profits on the loss leaders may be nil, but they hope the gross profit from all sales will be higher.

International. Anschluss, the union of Austria with Germany in 1938, provides a vivid example of negotiators (the Austrian government) working against their homeostatic need for survival. After World War I the great Austro-Hungarian Empire was divided and Austria became a minor power deprived of the economic resources it needed to survive. Although the Treaty of Versailles had forbidden union between Germany and Austria, sentiment for it grew every time Austria went through one of its periodic financial crises. Adolf Hitler's rise to power brought the threat of *Anschluss* nearer. For a time the National Socialist (Nazi) Party was banned in Austria because of its strident support of *Anschluss*. However, Chancellor Kurt von Schuschnigg (the opposer) was forced to legalize the Nazi Party and in 1938 to appoint three Nazis to high government offices. Now thoroughly alarmed by German threats, Schuschnigg called for a plebiscite on *Anschluss* and made a belated effort to unify his bitterly divided nation. Hitler's response was a demand that the plebiscite be called off, and German troops were massed at the Austrian border. Schuschnigg resigned. German troops occupied the country without resistance from the Austrian people, who then voted overwhelmingly for *Anschluss*. The Austrians (the negotiators) had traded their national identity for possible individual advantages.

5. NEGOTIATOR WORKS AGAINST THE OPPOSER'S HOMEOSTATIC NEEDS

Interpersonal. A simple example is the case of a woman (negotiator) on a sinking ship. She wants to get into the lifeboat, but there is a man (opposer) ahead of her. She negotiates for her own life by using a culturally accepted formula as a gambit. She states a law of the sea—"Women and children first." She works against the most basic need of the man—preservation of his life—in her attempt to have him step aside at his own mortal risk.

Interorganizational. In 1964 a federal panel headed by U.S. Surgeon General Luther Terry reported that smoking was definitely harmful to health. Most damning was medical evidence indicating that cigarettes, in particular, increased one's susceptibility to lung cancer. Although some measures were taken to control cigarette advertisements, smoking is still allowed to be advertised in magazines and newspapers.   When a cigarette advertiser (negotiator) shows a beautiful girl and an adoring swain enjoying a good smoke, the advertiser is working directly against the homeostatic survival needs of the public (the opposer).

International. Control of territory is one of the basic homeostatic needs of a state. The purchase of Florida in 1819 by the United States (the negotiator) from Spain (the opposer) illustrates the use of this gambit, not only of working against one's opponent's need but brazenly using the gambit as an argument to *justify* the giving up of territory. The negotiations began as a result of an invasion of Spanish-owned Florida by General Andrew Jackson. A band in Indians and runaway slaves living near Pensacola had been making raids along the Georgia border. Jackson had orders to drive them out of the United States; he did so and then swept into Spanish territory and captured Pensacola and St. Marks.

James Monroe's cabinet, with the exception of John Quincy Adams (the negotiator), voted to apologize to Spain (the opposer) and reprimand Jackson. Adams, then Secretary of State, condemned both proposals and won Monroe's support. In a tough ultimatum Adams told Spain (the opposer) that if it could not police Florida, it should cede the territory to the United States. Spain, which was embroiled with its own rebellious South American colonies, could offer neither armed resistance nor effective argument against Adams' gambit. After long negotiation, Florida was ceded to the United States for $5 million, and even that sum did not go to the Spanish government. It was used to pay outstanding debts owed by Spaniards to U.S. citizens.

6. Negotiator Works Against the Opposer's and His Own Homeostatic Needs

Interpersonal. A negotiated, joint (negotiator and opposer) suicide pact is an illustration of this type of gambit that carries finality.

Interorganizational. When a strike is called, each side (negotiator and opposer) from that time on gives up its homeostatic need. The supplies to the factories are cut off and the wages to the employees are stopped. The fact that a strike affects the homeostatic needs of both sides makes it a very strong negotiating gambit.

Of course, in some union-industry disputes the participants are the last to feel the economic strain. Industry merely pays less in taxes or receives a tax refund. Employees are able to receive unemployment insurance plus compensation from union funds.

International. The U.S. Embargo of 1807 provides a unique example. The French Revolutionary Wars, and the Napoleonic Wars that followed, brought the United States to the brink of war with either Great Britain or France on a number of occasions. The national feeling varied as first one nation and then the other committed new outrages against American merchant shipping. Britain was trying to shut off all neutral trade with France. Napoleon, under his Continental System, seized any ship that was trading with Great Britain. Numerous American ships were seized by both sides.

President Thomas Jefferson (the negotiator) tried a bold new approach—bold because U.S. revenue relied for the most part on import duties, new because no western nation had ever tried to shut off all commerce with all European nations (the opposers). The Embargo of 1807 did just that. No European ships were allowed to enter or leave American seaports. When it became apparent that trade continued with Britain through Canada, which was then its colony, Jefferson put an end to shipping on the American inland waterways as well.

Jefferson hoped that by depriving England and France of U.S. agricultural products and other trade he would work against their homeostatic need for food and clothing and force them into making concessions to the United States. He was also willing to sacrifice an even more basic national homeostatic need: sources of revenue. The gambit was disastrous to the United States. The American maritime fleet did not recover for many years. Shipbuilders and farmers suffered from the cutoff of international trade. And in two years U.S. revenues dropped to from $16 million in 1807 to $7 million in 1809. Jefferson had worked against his own country's need with a vengeance. Unfortunately he underestimated the homeostatic need for national self-survival that dominated British and French thinking. This was more important to both nations than commerce with the United States. In 1809, shortly before his second term ended, Jefferson reluctantly admitted the embargo was a failure and obtained congressional repeal of the act.

II. SAFETY AND SECURITY NEEDS

1. NEGOTIATOR WORKS FOR THE OPPOSER'S SAFETY AND SECURITY NEEDS

Interpersonal. The efforts that parents (the negotiators) may use to try to promote "desirable" marriages for their children (the opposers) is an example of this gambit. The appeal is directed toward the child's need for the security that the parents say wealth and social position will provide. At the parents' age this need seems more basic than the child's romantic aspirations.

Dr. Samuel Johnson's statement on this subject was considerably more blunt than anything today's wise parent would be likely to say: "Were I a man of rank, I would not let my daughter starve who had made a mean marriage, but having voluntarily degraded herself from the station she was originally entitled to hold, I would support her only in that which she herself had chosen. . . ." Note that Johnson's unforgiving attitude adds further force to this gambit.

Interorganizational. It is common for a modern corporation to work for the security of its employees. The corporation (negotiator) may do this by financing pension plans, by sharing its profits, or by giving large deferred bonuses to its employees (the opposers). The corporation may use its employees' need for economic security to encourage loyalty to the firm and better work. This negotiating gambit has become increasingly important in recent years in settling labor disputes, in obtaining new union contracts, and also in preventing unionization of an unorganized segment of the corporation.

International. On April 7, 1965, President Lyndon Johnson (the negotiator) offered to enter unconditional peace talks with North Vietnam, Communist China, and the Soviet Union to end the war in Vietnam. To persuade the Communist countries (the opposers) to agree, he used a negotiating gambit that was in marked contrast to the usual tactics of war. He urged all the countries in Southeast Asia, including North Vietnam, to undertake a massive cooperative development program. This program would be initiated by the United Nations and financed by all industrialized countries. He himself would ask Congress to appropriate $1 billion to the project as soon as it was under way. Although U.N. Secretary General U Thant praised Johnson's gambit as "positive, forward-looking, and generous," the Communist countries felt quite differently. "Stinks of poison gas," said Communist China, and within a week all three countries involved had rejected Johnson's efforts to work for his opposer's needs.

2. NEGOTIATOR LETS THE OPPOSER WORK FOR HIS SAFETY AND SECURITY NEEDS

Interpersonal. Captain John Smith (the negotiator), who led the English settlement at Jamestown in 1608, understood how to make the colonists work for their needs. In the colony's earliest days, the settlers (opposers) did not have the right to own land and property. Many were unwilling to spend long hours tilling fields they did not own—even though food was extremely scarce. John Smith countered their laziness by taking charge of all the food produced in the colony. He then issued a very simple order. All those who were well enough to work must work to get food. His maneuver worked and so did all the colonists.

Interorganizational. A truly remarkable example of forcing opposers to work for their security need was made by a client of mine. He was a wealthy Chicago philanthropist who had generously contributed his time and money to the field of heart research. He (the negotiator) was requested to testify before a Senate committee (the opposers) that was investigating the possibility of establishing a National Heart Foundation. The cause was one that he held dear and he consulted with the best experts to prepare his address. Private heart organizations worked with him, furnishing concise, well-documented appeals for presentation to the senators. Armed with this prepared speech, my client took his place in the hearing room, only to discover that he would be the sixth person to be called to testify. The five speakers who preceded him were outstanding professionals—medical men, scientists, and public relations men. These men had spent their lives at this work. The committee put them through their paces and at one point asked the witness before them, "Who wrote your speech for you?"

When my client was called, he stood before the senators and said, "Gentlemen, I had prepared a speech but I have discarded it. For how could I compete with the eminent men who have already spoken? They have given you all the facts and figures, but I am here to appeal to you on your own behalf. Hard-working men such as you are the victims of heart disease. You are men in the prime of your lives, at the top of your careers; you are just the ones most susceptible to heart attack. People who have achieved outstanding positions in their community are the ones most subject to heart disease."

He continued in this vein for forty-five minutes; they would not let him stop. He was making each senator work for his "need," his need of safety. The National Heart Foundation was thereafter created by the government, and my client was its first governor.

International. The deals that Iraq (the negotiator) made with foreign oil companies (the opposers) operating within Iraq illustrate an international negotiation in which the opposers were forced to work for their needs. In 1951 the ownership of the Iraq Petroleum Company was typical of the ownership of all the large oil companies in the country. Ninety-five per cent of the shares in the company were held by foreign interests—American, Dutch, French, and British. In negotiating a new deal with this foreign-held company, Iraq forced the company to work for its need to extract Iraq oil. The company agreed to give 50 per cent of its profits to Iraq. It also promised to work harder and to increase its oil production, further increasing the Iraqi government's oil revenue. The other foreign-held companies were soon forced to make the same concessions.

3. Negotiator Works for the Opposer's and His Own Safety and Security Needs

Interpersonal. Frontier days in the American West furnish a good example of people working for their need for safety and security and for their opposer's need as well. Invariably, as communities were founded and families moved in, the settlers (negotiators and opposers) demanded "law and order." Although their demands would mean giving up the absolute freedom the frontier afforded, the need for safety made the sacrifice worthwhile to most people in the community.

Interorganizational. The "common enemy" gambit has often persuaded opposing organizations to work together for their own security. The threat of an outside force, either real or imaginary, makes their differences seem less important. Political parties, especially in Europe, are very dependent on this negotiating gambit. For example, in 1964 the Italian Christian Democrats (the negotiators) made a dramatic opening to the Left and allied with the left-wing Socialists, the Democratic Socialists, and the Republicans (the opposers). This alliance was prompted by the power of the Communist Party in Italy, one of the strongest Communist parties outside the Soviet Bloc.

International. The International Monetary Fund, set up at the U.N. Monetary and Financial Conference at Bretton Woods in 1944, works to stabilize the currencies of all member countries. Each nation (negotiator and opposer) that joins the IMF agrees to contribute to a foreign exchange reserve. The Fund can then draw on this reserve to help any member during a temporary balance-of-payments crisis. Many of the members of the Fund compete with each other for markets in international trade. Yet it is to their advantage to help their competitors indirectly through the International Monetary Fund. By supporting a weak currency, even the currency of a competitor, they help prevent an international financial crisis and protect their own economic security.

4. Negotiator Works Against His Safety and Security Needs

Interpersonal. Playwright Arthur Miller (negotiator) worked against his own need for security in a drama that was only too real. Called to testify before the House Un-American Activities Committee (opposers) in 1956, the Pulitzer Prize playwright was willing to answer all questions relating to his own political experience and affiliations. Never a member of the Communist Party himself, he could expect to emerge from the investigation safe and sound. However, the Committee wanted information not just about Miller's own experience, but concerning his friends and associates as well. This he refused to divulge. To protect others, he jeopardized his own security. His negotiating gambit failed. A federal district court convicted him of contempt of Congress the next year.

Interorganizational. A military maneuver in common use during the early Middle Ages furnishes an example of working against the need for safety. The defenders of a fort (the negotiators), under attack by a besieging army (the opposers), made it a practice to sally forth and give battle to the attackers. As they crossed the moat they burned the bridge behind them. By thus cutting off their only means of retreat, they served notice on their enemy that they never intended to reenter the fort again unless they were victorious. Their purpose was to inspire fear in the hearts of the besieging army. The defenders gave up their need for safety and apparently committed an irrational act, but it often proved to be an effective means of negotiation. This is the origin of the expression "burning your bridges behind you."

International. In 1936 General Francisco Franco led a revolt against the Republican government of Spain. Supported by the Spanish clergy, nobility, and Army, he won control of vast parts of western and northern Spain in a matter of months. Germany and Italy came to his aid. France and Britain decided not to intervene. Only Russia officially helped the Republicans. However, thousands of individuals from all over the world came to Spain and fought on the side of those loyal to the Republican cause. The International Brigade made up of these volunteers was a key to the successful defense of Madrid and of Spain. In 1937 Franco continued his conquest of the north, and in 1938 he drove south to the Mediterranean at Vinaroz to split Republican Spain. Again aided by the International Brigade, the Loyalists mounted a desperate counter-offensive and succeeded in recapturing the southern bank of the Ebro River. The Republican government (the negotiator) tried to use this victory to persuade Franco (the opposer) to negotiate peace terms. To prove his good will, Don Juan Negrin, Premier of Spain, worked against the security of his government. He sent the International Brigade home. Negrin's maneuver failed, Franco continued his offensive, and the Republican government fell.

It is possible for a nation to achieve more successful results by using the negotiation gambit of giving up its own safety. In 1940, early in World War II, the Germans invaded Denmark. For a time no move was made against the Danish Jews. Then one day in 1943, after the Danish underground had intensified its sabotage against the Nazis, the Germans decreed that all Jews in Denmark must wear a yellow arm band with a Star of David. Similar decrees had marked Jews for deportation to concentration camps, country after country, all across Europe. That night the Danish underground relayed a message throughout Denmark. King Christian X had announced that each Dane was the same as every other Dane and he himself would wear the first Star of David. He expected all Danes to follow his example. The next day in Copenhagen almost everyone wore the Star of David. King Christian's negotiating gambit worked, the Germans rescinded their order, and the Danish Jews survived.

5. Negotiator Works Against the Opposer's Safety and Security Needs

Interpersonal. If properly used, the "dare" can prove a very effective negotiating technique. Children appear to use it instinctively. The negotiator works against an opposer's need for safety and security by goading him into a dangerous act, or one that at least seems to threaten his need for safety and security.

Interorganizational. Nowadays armies have psychologists to help soldiers face the peril of war. They (the negotiators) explain to the soldiers (the opposers) that it is perfectly normal to be afraid and that the real problem is to learn not to be afraid of being afraid. In this fashion the psychologists persuade the soldiers to overcome their fear, to bear arms willingly, and to work against their need for safety. Abraham Lincoln (the negotiator) used this gambit to rally the North behind him at the outbreak of the Civil War. South Carolina had demanded the surrender of Fort Sumter, which guarded Charleston harbor. Lincoln refused to surrender the fort, saying it would violate the oath he had taken as President to protect federal property. He also stated that he would send unarmed supply ships to the fort but that they were to turn back if South Carolina offered resistance. The fiery Confederate general P. G. T. Beauregard (the opposer) did not wait for the confrontation. He fired on the fort and forced its surrender. Thus he gave Lincoln the priceless advantage of appearing as the defender of the Union rather than the aggressor against Southern liberties, as the South had portrayed him.

International. In 1917 Germany (the negotiator) effectively worked against the security of one of its opposers, Russia, in World War I. As Winston Churchill describes it:

> In the middle of April the Germans took a sombre decision.
> Ludendorff refers to it with bated breath. Full allowance must
> be made for the desperate stakes to which the German leaders
> were already committed. They were in the mood which had
> opened unlimited submarine warfare with the certainty of
> bringing the United States into the war against them. Upon
> the western front they had from the beginning used the most
> terrible means of offense at their disposal. They had employed
> poison gas on the largest scale and had invented the "Flam-
> menwerfer" (flame-thrower). Nevertheless, it was with a sense

of awe that they turned upon Russia the most grisly of all weapons. They transported Lenin in a sealed truck like a plague bacillus from Switzerland into Russia.

Lenin was living in exile in Switzerland when a revolt in Russia forced Czar Nicholas II to abdicate his throne in March 1917. Lenin's desire to end Russian participation in an "imperialist war" and to begin an internal "class war" was well known to the Germans. By allowing Lenin to return to Russia, the Germans worked against their opposer's need for a stable government. As expected, once in Russia, Lenin increased the power and influence of the Bolsheviks and overthrew the provisional government in a second revolution. Russia's war effort suffered as a result of its internal problem. In addition, in 1918, as chairman of the Council of People's Commissars, Lenin sued for an early peace with Germany.

6. Negotiator Works Against the Opposer's and His Own Safety and Security Needs

Interpersonal. In the game of Russian roulette each individual (negotiator and opposer) negotiates against the safety need of both parties. This gruesome game is reputed to have settled many a negotiation impasse in days of old. It is played by placing only one bullet in the chamber of a six-shooter, spinning the barrel, and then passing the revolver to each player in turn. Each player takes the gun, holds it to his head, and pulls the trigger. Chance gives the winner life.

Teen-agers have devised their own form of Russian roulette in their game called "chicken." Starting some distance apart, two cars are driven toward each other, each car straddling the center white line of the road and going as fast as the courage or foolhardiness of the drivers will allow. The first driver to veer off the white line to escape collision is taunted as being "chicken," or coward.

Interorganizational. The crusade for civil rights in the South has seen many examples of organizations and groups (the negotiators) working against their needs and those of their opposers. Sometimes the economic security of only a few people is affected when a baseball park closes to avoid integration. Other times the loss of economic security affects many when schools close and children are not educated for future jobs and responsibilities. And in still other cases a whole community, Klansmen as well as members of CORE, lose economic security when riots against integration cancel plans for financial investment in the area.

International. A motion picture, *Dr. Strangelove*, suggests a fictional example of a nation working against its need for security and the need of its opposers. In the film one nation (the negotiator) had invented a "Doomsday" machine capable of incalculable destruction. The nation could conceivably use its superinvention to negotiate with the rest of the world (the opposer) by threatening to destroy itself and the entire world in the event of an attack. In this way it would be negotiating against its own safety and the safety of all its opposers.

Before the United States and the Soviet Union agreed to ban testing nuclear weapons above ground, increased radioactivity in the air presented a very real threat to the safety of all. SANE, an organization dedicated to working *for* the world's security, described the situation in an advertisement that read as follows: "We now have enough atom bombs to kill every Russian 360 times. The Russians only have enough atom bombs to kill every American 150 times. We're ahead. Aren't we?"

III. LOVE AND BELONGING NEEDS

1. NEGOTIATOR WORKS FOR THE OPPOSER'S LOVE AND BELONGING NEEDS

Interpersonal. One day, while commuting to New York City, I had a conversation with a neighbor. Our discussion serves as a good example of working for the opposer's need for love and belonging. He asked what I was working on. I explained that I was writing a book on the art of negotiating.

"Oh, I negotiate all the time in my business," exclaimed my fellow traveler. "I buy up distressed lots of textiles and, in my opinion, there's *only one way* to negotiate." He explained his method.

"I have to get the merchandise at the lowest possible price, so I have found that the *best* way is to knock the quality and run it down. I often let the goods fall on the floor and then step on it accidently. After downgrading the merchandise, I make some ridiculous offer. Then we usually haggle a bit and close the deal."

I listened attentively and then said, "I disagree with your use of the phrase 'only one way.' Might I suggest at least one alternative approach, just the reverse of what you do? Your method, while useful, might create an antagonistic feeling, especially when you knock down fabrics that a man has spent his time, talent, and money to design and produce. People feel paternal toward things that are theirs. We speak with pride of *my* *h*ouse, *my* car. How would you feel if somebody started knocking your house or your car? Now suppose you are the seller, showing me a fabric. As another gambit, I might say, 'The pattern is lovely but I think your design is ahead of the current market. Of course, if you hold the goods for about ten years, I think the taste of the general public will catch up with your ideas.' Without knocking the merchandise I have put it into an unfavorable position. The seller is certainly made more anxious to sell now when faced with the prospect of waiting ten years for the goods to become marketable. He knows it is not marketable or he would be offering the goods to the regular trade. I (the negotiator) have worked on his (the opposer's) need for love and belonging to reach agreement. Belonging can apply to things as well as to people. When we have concluded the deal, the seller will also be more likely to ship me some of the material in the best condition rather than the worst lot."

This attachment to things that are ours is very deep-seated and is well summed up by Shakespeare in the phrase, "a poor thing, but mine own."

Interorganizational. "If you can't beat 'em, join 'em" is an old adage. It has proved a useful gambit for the negotiator to work for his opposer's need to belong by joining the opposer's forces. The epic battle among the railroad kings at the turn of the century provides a multiple illustration of the point. Three great financiers were involved: J. P. Morgan, who was financing a reorganization of the Northern Pacific; James J. Hill, who held a controlling interest in the Great Northern; and Edward H. Harriman, who controlled the Union Pacific. All three wanted control of the Chicago, Burlington, and Quincy. It would give Morgan and Hill entrance into Chicago and St. Louis, but it would give Harriman access to the Northeast.

Hill and Morgan—working against Harriman—combined to buy a controlling interest in the C. B. & Q. Then they split control of the road between their two companies. But Harriman was not a man to be thwarted. He turned around and bought enough of Northern Pacific's common and preferred stock to give him control of that railroad and also of its 50 per cent interest in the C.B. & Q. Hill and his friends postponed the annual meeting of the Northern Pacific in order to retire the preferred stock and destroy Harriman's majority before he could elect a new board. All these maneuvers brought on the panic of May 9, 1901, when those who had sold short could not buy Northern Pacific stock even at $1,000 a share. The three rivals had had enough. They combined to form a holding company, the Northern Securities Company, to act as trustee for the Northern Pacific, the Great Northern, and the C. B. & Q. Harriman was given minority representation on its board.

That is not the end of the story. Later we shall see how Morgan attempted to use the gambit once more, this time with the President of the United States. Theodore Roosevelt was a match for the financier, he turned the gambit around and used it against Morgan.

International. Harry S. Truman's Point Four Program is an example of one nation working for the need of underdeveloped nations to belong. Truman (the negotiator) proposed the program in his 1949 inaugural address. He offered to share American technical skills, knowledge, and equipment with underdeveloped nations (the opposers) to improve their industries, agriculture, health, and education. The program also encouraged Americans to invest private funds in these countries. Point Four worked for the belonging need of the participating nations: by assisting their development, it gave them entrée to the ranks of the modern industrial nations.

2. NEGOTIATOR LETS THE OPPOSER WORK FOR HIS LOVE AND BELONGING NEEDS

Interpersonal. Just as a sentry on guard duty forces an unknown person to identify himself, so you, as a negotiator, can make other people identify themselves to you. If you listen carefully to what people say, you will find that "between the lines" of their conversation they are explaining their various needs for love and belonging. They tell you how nice they are, how their goals and aims are the same as yours. To use this as a gambit of negotiation, you (the negotiator) permit them (the opposer) to fulfill their need for love and belonging through you. Listen carefully to what they say and then act so that they fulfill their needs.

Another example of this gambit is the social club (negotiator) that enforces various types of restrictions on membership. It forces any prospective member (opposer) to work hard for his need to belong. It is, therefore, not odd that clubs with easier membership requirements sometimes find it more difficult to fill their roster than do clubs with stiffer demands.

Interorganizational. The New York Stock Exchange (the negotiator) uses this gambit very effectively. Before a corporation (the opposer) will be listed on the Big Board, it must file an extremely detailed statement of the company's affairs. Thereafter, it must make regular reports to the Exchange on its earnings and general financial situation. There are a number of reasons why a corporation might not wish to reveal this information, but the need for belonging outweighs them in many cases and a listing is eagerly sought, because when the Exchange lists a stock, it in effect endorses the company's status.

International. After World War II, the United States and its allies (the negotiators) forced Japan (the opposer) to work for its need to belong to the family of nations. Although the Japanese government continued to function throughout the occupation, it was denied full sovereignty until it enacted a broad program of political, economic, and social reforms. After seven years, during which the reforms became firmly embedded in Japanese life, the Allies granted Japan full sovereignty.

3. Negotiator Works for the Opposer's and His Own Love and Belonging Needs

Interpersonal. A real estate broker I know, in his capacity as agent in name and fact, uses this gambit effectively. He puts the gambit into operation by telling the prospective buyer that the seller feels that he is just the type of person to whom he would like to sell his home. Then the broker works on the seller, telling him all the nice things the buyer said in response to the seller's compliment. Naturally, when he brings the two together they are extremely cordial. The broker's negotiating tactic has created a feeling of belonging between seller (negotiator) and buyer (opposer). Usually the final closing of the deal goes quickly and smoothly.

Interorganizational. In the business community it is common practice to join associations in which competitors (negotiator and

opposer) can work together toward a common goal. This might
be done to secure legislation that will favor the industry as a whole
—or to fight against unfavorable legislation. The goal may also be to
share common experiences and problems encountered in the industry.

At future labor conventions it might well be a good idea to provide for displays, parades, floats, all graphically demonstrating what
the workers and the industries produce together. The higher level
of achievement, of belonging, is lost to union and management
when there are protracted struggles for the more basic needs. Cooperative long-term possibilities are perverted by the immediate
goals that both labor and management strive for.

International. Great Britain (negotiator), in setting up the Commonwealth of Nations, worked for its own belonging need and that
of its former colonies (opposers). Although the Commonwealth
ties are rather tenuous, there are definite advantages to be derived
by all member nations. This was underlined by the extreme re-
luctance shown by South Africa to withdraw from the Commonwealth in 1961. The fact that it did withdraw again illustrates that
an appeal to the more basic need will usually carry the day.

South Africa became a republic in 1960. It applied for readmis-
sion to the Commonwealth, which required the approval of the
other members. South Africa had aroused great resentment because
of its repressive racial policies directed against Indians as well as
Africans. The basic argument for this policy was that it would save
the white minority government from being taken over by Africans
and Asians. In the face of vehement criticism from the Asian Commonwealth members, South Africa withdrew its application for re-
admission. Its need for security had proved stronger than its belonging need.

4. NEGOTIATOR WORKS AGAINST HIS LOVE AND BELONGING NEEDS

Interpersonal. Children (the negotiators) often negotiate in
their endless fights with grown-ups (the opposers) by using the
gambit of giving up their need for love and belonging. There is the
story of the child who decided he wasn't being treated properly at
home and therefore was going to run away. He packed his things
and left a note behind: "I am running away from home. I will
never come back. In the case of an air raid, I can be found in the
attic." The boy was willing to give up his need for belonging, but

was not so annoyed that he would give up his security need.

Interorganizational. The Protestant Reformation in Germany provides numerous examples of working against one's need for belonging. It might properly be used as an example on the personal, organizational, and international level. However, since Germany was divided into many principalities and free cities united only by their allegiance to the Church and their loose ties with the Holy Roman Empire, perhaps this example best exemplifies the inter-organizational level of approach.

For 1,500 years a common faith and the Catholic Church had been almost the only unifying force in Europe. It is difficult today to realize the agonizing choice that faced Martin Luther and his followers (negotiators): to remain in the Church (opposer), which seemed to them venal and corrupt, or to give up their membership in a religious community that embraced most of Europe. There were political and economic, as well as spiritual, reasons that brought half the inhabitants of Germany over to Protestantism, but in any event the choice was a bitter one to make.

International. When France and Germany entered the Common Market, agreement was soon reached concerning free trade in industrial goods. But the treaty provisions in agriculture were vague, far vaguer than the detailed schedule for industrial free trade. Germany wanted to maintain the unsettled state of the agricultural schedules because it benefited the German farmers. On the other hand, during four years of discussion and debate, the French pressed for a common policy on farm products similar in detail and precision to the policy on industrial products; this was what the French farmers needed and wanted. Tired of the stalling tactics of the Germans, the French issued a threat: if Germany did not go through with the original understanding on farm prices by a certain date, France would withdraw from the Common Market. Thus the French (negotiators) were working against their need for belonging in order to negotiate the Germans (opposers) into a satisfactory agreement on the farm schedules.

5. NEGOTIATOR WORKS AGAINST THE OPPOSER'S LOVE AND BELONGING NEEDS

Interpersonal. Earlier in this chapter I gave an example of working for the opposer's need for belonging, in my conversation with my commuting friend. It is sometimes advantageous to take the negative approach and work against the opposer's need for love and belonging. When negotiating to buy an article, you (the negotiator) devalue it by finding fault with the quality. This gambit is used in purchasing used clothes; the buyer often points out rips, tears, or stains, or holds the seat of the pants up to the light so the seller (opposer) and he can see the almost inevitable worn-out places.

Negotiating the purchase of a house, the potential buyer often calls attention to defective plumbing, a bad roof, or other faults. Some people feel that this will make the owner give up his need for belonging—at least in reference to the article for sale.

Interorganizational. The boycott by the Arab nations (the negotiators) of U.S. companies (opposers) dealing with Israel is an example of this gambit on the interorganizational level. It has a double impact that few realize. If the American company continues to trade with Israel, it gives up its Arab market. However, if it complies with the Arab demand to prove it has not traded with Israel, the company is demonstrating weakness: it is giving up, to a degree, its sense of belonging to a powerful and independent nation (the United States).

International. Working against the opposer's need for belonging and love has been given various names, such as the phrase "sent to Coventry." On the international level, this has been done to Red China, which has been kept out of the United Nations. The more Red China (the opposer) tried to work its way in, the more the United States (negotiator) has negotiated to keep it out. The United States' position is that Communist China must earn its place in the family of nations by proper actions before it can be admitted. The United States is working here against China's desire to belong (not to the U.N., but to the civilized world). China, however, has taken the understandable position of claiming no interest in a U.N. seat, even if one is offered.

6. NEGOTIATOR WORKS AGAINST THE OPPOSER'S AND HIS OWN LOVE AND BELONGING NEEDS

Interpersonal. In the last scene of Shakespeare's *Romeo and Juliet*, the Prince (agent) brings about peace between the Capulets (negotiators) and the Montagues (opposers). With both Romeo and Juliet dead, the Prince wants both families to work against their individual needs to belong. He tells them:

> *See, what a scourge is laid upon your hate,*
> *That Heaven finds means to kill your joys with love,*
> *And I for winking at your discords too*
> *Have lost a brace of kinsmen. All are punish'd.*

The Prince recognizes that each party gave up its need for love in losing a member of its family, and he uses this fact to make them acknowledge their folly and agree to negotiate peace.

Interorganizational. Hill and Morgan's Northern Securities Company has already been used as an example of working for the opponent's belonging need. Subsequent developments show that it is a good example of working *against* the belonging need. In 1902 President Theodore Roosevelt (the negotiator) ordered his Attorney General to enter a suit to dissolve the holding company, Northern Securities Company. J. P. Morgan (the opposer) and other major contributors to the President's Republican Party hurried to Washington to talk Rooosevelt out of it. Morgan suggested to Roosevelt the time-honored solution of working together: "If we have done anything wrong, send your man to my man and they can fix it up."

As Roosevelt observed later, "That is a most illuminating illustration of the Wall Street point of view. Mr. Morgan could not help regarding me as a big rival operator, who either intended to ruin all his interests, or else could be induced to come to an agreement to ruin none."

This attitude did not suit the superpatriot Roosevelt. Duty to country came before any need for Wall Street support in the forthcoming 1904 election. Therefore he worked against his and Morgan's belonging need in order to protect "the interests of the people against monopoly and privilege . . ." The gambit worked. The Supreme Court ordered the breaking up of the Northern Securities Company, and although Wall Street tried to prevent his nomination in 1904, Roosevelt won the nomination and was re-elected by the American people whose interests he had defended.

International. From the time of the creation of Malaysia in 1963, Indonesia had attempted to destroy the federation, using diplomatic pressure and guerrilla warfare. The United States attempted to force Indonesia into line by threatening to withdraw its aid to the Asian country. By 1964 aid had virtually ceased, and Indonesia (the negotiator) declared it did not want aid from countries (opposers) that did not support its Malaysian policy. In 1965 Indonesia also worked against its own and its opposer's need to belong when it withdrew from the United Nations, which had just elected Malaysia to the Security Council.

IV. ESTEEM NEEDS

1. Negotiator Works for the Opposer's Esteem Needs

Interpersonal. Sometimes you (negotiator) will find it advantageous to work for your opposer's need of esteem by becoming sincerely interested and involved with him. Dale Carnegie, in *How to Win Friends and Influence People*, describes many applications of this principle. Some of the methods he advocates are: become genuinely interested in people, smile, always remember that a man's name is the most important sound to him, encourage others to talk about themselves, talk in terms of the other fellow's interests, and strive to make the other person feel important. All these forms of conversing with your opposer feed his basic need for esteem, and when properly applied they are valuable assets in the art of negotiation.

Interorganizational. Modern corporations constantly work to obtain public esteem and goodwill. One corporation may use another corporation's need for public esteem to serve its own advantage. For example, a few years ago the Xerox Corporation wanted to extend its operations into England and other European countries. It therefore joined J. Arthur Rank, Ltd., a well-known English firm, and formed a new company, Rank-Xerox, to promote its products in Europe. By working for Xerox's (opposer's) need for public esteem in Europe, J. Arthur Rank (negotiator) gained the right to profit from the industrial processes Xerox had developed.

International. Nations traditionally indicate their acceptance of a change in leadership in another country by formally recognizing the new government. For some time following the Russian Revolution of 1917, no nation recognized the U.S.S.R. The United States based its refusal to recognize Russia on several factors: the U.S.S.R. refused to assume the financial obligations incurred by the Czarist government, refused to recognize claims of American citizens for losses incurred during the revolution, and refused to end subversive activities against the governments of other countries. By 1933 the desire to increase American trade with the U.S.S.R. superseded these objections. Ignoring most American claims against the Soviet Union, Franklin D. Roosevelt (negotiator) worked for Russia's (opposer's) need for esteem and formally extended diplomatic recognition on November 16, 1933.

2. Negotiator Lets the Opposer Work for His Esteem Needs

Interpersonal. An opposer commonly works for his need for esteem during negotiations prior to a divorce. For example, a model husband (negotiator) may allow his errant wife (opposer) to sue him for a divorce. Thus he is protecting her reputation and in return she is forced to work for her need for public esteem by offering him a better property settlement, better custody arrangements or, at the very least, peace and quiet.

Interorganizational. An employer (negotiator) can profitably encourage his employees (opposers) to work for their need for esteem. The employer sets up an award to honor the individual or division with the best record for attendance or production or any other kind of behavior he wants to encourage. The employees then exert themselves to win the recognition the award conveys. Perhaps the most famous employer to use this negotiating gambit is the Soviet Union. Production problems in 1935 led Stalin to call for all Soviet workers to produce more. One coal miner named Stakhanov surprised even Stalin by exceeding his quota several times over. Stalin, therefore, proclaimed 1936 as "Stakhanov year." All workers who succeeded in becoming Stakhanovites received not only awards but special privileges and bonuses as well.

International. The United States recognized the Soviet Union in 1933 with a few strings attached, but it had used a far different negotiating gambit in dealing with Mexico in 1913. Until that time the United States had usually recognized established governments as a matter of course, no matter how these governments came into power. However, in 1913 Victoriano Huerta organized a bloody coup against the government of Francisco Madero, the first Mexican government in many years that had sought to bring prosperity to the masses and political liberties to all Mexicans. Madero himself lost his life while in Huerta's custody. Although many countries established diplomatic relations with the Huerta government (opposer) at once, U.S. President Woodrow Wilson (negotiator) refused to recognize "government by murder." He went even further and insisted that the price for U.S. esteem was Huerta's resignation. Wilson's decision cost American investors in Mexico tens of thousand of dollars every day. The German Kaiser remarked, "Morality is all right, but what about dividends?" Dividends notwithstanding, Wilson persisted in his policy, eventually supplying arms to Huerta's enemies and finally sending in American troops. No longer able to resist U.S. pressure, Huerta went into voluntary exile.

3. Negotiator Works for the Opposer's and His Own Esteem Needs

Interpersonal. Sometimes all that is necessary to effect a successful negotiation between the negotiator and opposer is a gambit that will allow both parties to work for their need for esteem and to save face. One of the most common face-saving gambits is for each side to talk separately with a third, neutral party. By granting concessions to such a moderator rather than directly to each other, each party works for his need for esteem.

Interorganizational. Competing corporations sometimes work for each other's need for esteem by forming an industrial association. The association works to enhance the reputation of the entire industry, often with the help of a public relations firm hired jointly by all the firms through the association. "Together great things can be accomplished" could be the title of this gambit, which is used by competitors (negotiators and opposers) in industries ranging from ribbon to steel.

International. One of the most famous and enduring examples of nations working together to build mutual esteem is the Olympic Games. The range of contests is wide so as to touch the skills of many nations. Small nations can hope to win esteem in competitions against large ones. For example, in the 1964 Olympics, New Zealand, Ethiopia, Finland, Romania, Switzerland, and Norway were among those winning athletic events.

4. Negotiator Works Against His Esteem Needs

Interpersonal. To work against your own need for esteem would seem to be an inconceivable method of negotiating. Nevertheless, this is exactly the technique that is used by a lawyer (negotiator) who is about to be held in contempt of court by a judge (opposer). In such a situation the lawyer often finds it expedient to apologize, beg for forgiveness, or assume a "country-boy" naiveté to explain his wrongdoing. In order to negotiate successfully with the judge, he deliberately debases himself and works against his need for esteem.

Interorganizational. Speakers (negotiators) at Alcoholics Anonymous use this gambit to persuade other drinkers (opposers) to give up the habit. The speakers work against their own need for esteem, confess to their past misdeeds, and tell what positive benefits abstinence offers the alcoholic.

International. After World War II, West Germany (the negotiator) adopted a severe attitude in prosecuting its war criminals, to show the world that it repudiated its Nazi past. By giving up its need for esteem it hoped to rejoin the Free World (opposer) as an equal partner.

5. Negotiator Works Against the Opposer's Esteem Needs

Interpersonal. By working against a person's need for esteem, you can cause that person to do many things. As an example, a father (negotiator) may teach his son (opposer) the family business and humility at the same time, by having him start at the bottom of the ladder. He is working against his son's need for esteem so that the son can acquire a full understanding of the business.

Interorganizational. When a fraternity (the negotiator) makes new pledges (the opposers) go through initiations that often degrade them and make them look ridiculous, they are negotiating against the esteem need of the prospective members. Similarly, the U.S. Army "negotiates" a man from a civilian into a soldier by putting him through a stiff course of basic training that works against his esteem need. But once he becomes a private first class, he has worked to recover his esteem as a soldier, with interest.

International. When the United States (the negotiator) publicizes economic failures in the Soviet Union, in Communist China, or in Cuba, the United States is working against its opposers' need for esteem. An unfriendly power similarly worked against America's need for esteem early in the nineteenth century. When James Madison became President in 1809, David Erskine was the British minister to Washington. Erskine had an American wife and was conciliatory to the U.S. need for esteem in every way. He and Madison negotiated an agreement to withdraw the British Orders in Council against American trade with France, in return for a number of concessions. These concessions did not satisfy George Canning, the British foreign minister. Canning not only refused to recognize his minister's agreement but replaced Erskine with a stern ultra-Britisher, "Copenhagen" Jackson. "Copenhagen" had earned his nickname by presenting the ultimatum that preceded Britain's seizure of the Danish fleet in 1807. He was even more contemputous of America's need for esteem than of Denmark's. He called Madison a "plain and rather mean-looking man." Madison's wife Dolly was "fat and forty, but not fair." Americans were "all alike" and "by many degrees more blackguard and ferocious than the mob in other countries." In line with Canning's intentions, Jackson proceeded to drive a hard bargain with the United States. He even accused the United States of acting in bad faith during the Erskine negotiations. But the British gambit boomeranged. Instead of knuckling under to Jackson's demands, U.S. Secretary of State Robert Smith refused to have any more dealings with the unpopular British minister.

6. Negotiator Works Against the Opposer's and His Own Esteem Needs

Interpersonal. A boy and a girl, out on their first date, can get involved in a negotiating situation, as unromantic as that term may sound. Because it is her first date with the boy, the girl may act according to an accepted code. If the boy wants to go further than she does, she negotiates to have him drop the request on the grounds that it is their first date. She (the negotiator) has worked against her own esteem need and also against the boy's (the opposer's). However, it is to be hoped that she has negotiated him into a second date.

Interorganizational. Labor-management disputes are often settled by both the negotiator and opposer giving up their need for esteem. If management yields to labor, it loses esteem by having given in. If union negotiators yield to management, they have the same difficulty. Yet to reach a settlement it is often necessary for both opposers to compromise and yield to the demands of the other. There is a saying: "It is not a good settlement unless both parties are a little bloody."

International. Before India received its freedom from Britain it adopted a policy of nonviolence toward the British. The Indians (negotiators) gave up their need of esteem but at the same time they also forced the British (opposer) into giving up their need for esteem. In following their policy of nonviolence and noncooperation, the Indians were often put into degrading situations that meant the loss of esteem. On the other hand the British, in attempting to enforce the law, were driven to harsh measures against a nonresistant people. This naturally worked against *their* need for esteem.

V. NEEDS FOR SELF-ACTUALIZATION

1. NEGOTIATOR WORKS FOR THE OPPOSER'S SELF-ACTUALIZATION NEEDS

Interpersonal. This gambit is typified by the wife (negotiator) who tells her husband (opposer), "OK, you can be boss." Whether she means it or not is beside the point. This is her negotiating technique. She may have strong convictions of what should be done, but she is not tipping her hand. She is playing on her husband's need for self-actualization, his inner need to develop his manly capacities. However, having granted her husband this privilege, she will expect concessions in return. There is the woman who brought harmony to her marriage by using the proven technique of permitting her husband to make all the big decisions: Should the United States stay out of foreign entanglements? Is a trip to the planets necessary for national security? She is content to make the small decisions: how the family income should be spent, or where they should spend their vacation.

In a confidence game in which the victim or mark is being set up to turn over a large sum of money to the con man, it is a rule of the game that the mark, not the con man, suggests handing over the money. The professional con man sets up the swindle so that the only logical result would be for the money to be turned over to him. However, the suggestion (motivation, self-actualization) must come from the victim.

Interorganizational. Large foundations (negotiators) often work for the self-actualization need of charitable and cultural organizations (opposers) by offering to match, dollar for dollar, any amount that is raised from other sources. This encourages the organizations to work harder at fund raising, of course doubles the impact of the foundation's program of creative giving, and enables the charity to develop to a fuller potential.

International. The "invention" of Panama, as it has been called, is an extreme example of the use of this gambit on the international level. In 1902, at about the time President Theodore Roosevelt (negotiator) had decided that the isthmus of Panama was the best place to dig a canal, Panama was a part of Colombia. But that country balked at giving the United States sovereignty over the necessary strip of land. Raging against "those contemptible little creatures in Bogotá," Roosevelt tacitly encouraged a revolution in Panama, and in November 1903 he sent three U.S. warships to prevent the landing of Colombian troops on the isthmus "if" revolution should break out.

The farce was over in a day. On November 3, the State Department wired the U.S. Consul in Panama: "Uprising on Isthmus reported. Keep Department promptly and fully informed." The consul replied that, alas, there had been no uprising yet but one was expected later that day. It happened on schedule and the Republic of Panama (opposer) was born. By working for the self-actualization need of the Panamanians (opposers), Roosevelt (negotiator) got exactly what he wanted: the most advantageous terms for building the Panama Canal.

2. NEGOTIATOR LETS THE OPPOSER WORK FOR HIS SELF-ACTUALIZATION NEEDS

Interpersonal. By letting the opposer work for his need for self-actualization you will give him a great degree of satisfaction (assuming that he is successful). In some situations you will find that you can negotiate better by offering your opposer a tough job, one difficult to accomplish, rather that an easy assignment. Winston Churchill (negotiator), in his famous statement, "I have nothing to offer but blood, toil, tears and sweat," was offering the British people (opposers) a hard task whose accomplishment would fulfill, among other needs, their need for self-actualization.

If in this and other examples used in this book the term "opposer" seems excessive, consider Churchill's bitter account of his party's defeat in the 1945 elections: "At the outset of this mighty battle, I acquired the chief power in the State . . . all of my enemies having surrendered. . . . I was immediately dismissed by the British electorate from all further conduct of their affairs." As any successful politician knows, the voters are his opposers; he must constantly negotiate with them if he is to stay in power.

Interorganizational. Industrial incentive plans and programs, where the employee has opportunities to perform in different capacities, work on the need of the employee (opposer) to feel that he can accomplish something worthwhile, that he can be important to the industry (negotiator)—in other words, they depend on his need for self-actualization. Many of the plans for redevelopment and slum clearance depend for their success on their ability to motivate the people in the depressed areas to join in the fight for neighborhood improvement. Here again we have the need for self-actualization.

International. Adolf Hitler (negotiator) made Great Britain and France (opposers) work for their self-actualization need in 1938 when he forced them to sign the Munich pact. The complacent democracies were willing to sacrifice their ally Czechoslovakia in exchange for "peace in our time," a peace that would ensure their complete freedom and domination over vast colonial empires. Only gradually did the democracies realize that they were exchanging the illusion of *self-actualization* for the more basic need of national survival.

3. Negotiator Works for the Opposer's and His Own Self-Actualization Needs

Interpersonal. The success of the jury system is dependent on the constant use of this gambit. It is axiomatic that no two persons think alike, yet Anglo-Saxon law assumes that twelve persons can reach an agreement most of the time. A conscientious juror will attempt to make his opinion prevail in order to achieve self-actualization. However, he (negotiator) cannot force the other jurors (opposers) to agree with him. He must negotiate with them, treat their opinions with respect, and arrive at a verdict that each juror can claim as his own.

Interorganizational. We are apt to think that the interests of the employer and his employees are divergent and opposed. However, during the stress of World War II, these diverse interests were often brought into accord. United in the effort to step up production for the defense of the country, employer and employees worked together in defense plants. Each party (negotiator and opposer) subordinated its own interests to the accomplishments of a greater task: winning the war. Both parties worked for their joint needs. In negotiations both the employers and the unions called each other's attention to their greater purpose. Under the pressure of war, the need for self-actualization of both parties was changed from monetary gains to a fervent patriotism. Even in peacetime a proper identification of mutual goals in the economic world will also bring employee and employer together. Some European nations, Sweden for instance, have peaceful labor relations based on this very gambit.

International. There has probably never been a more eloquent plea for opponents to work for self-actualization than that of Abraham Lincoln's second inaugural address. The end of the Civil War was in sight when Lincoln addressed both North and South (negotiator and opposer): "With malice toward none, with charity for all; with firmness in the right, as God has given us to see the right, let us strive on to finish the work that we are in; to bind up the nation's wounds; to care for him who shall have borne the battle, and for his widow, and his orphan—to do all which may achieve and cherish a just, and a lasting peace, among ourselves, and with all nations."

4. NEGOTIATOR WORKS AGAINST HIS SELF-ACTUALIZATION NEEDS

Interpersonal. The great Negro educator Booker T. Washington (negotiator) used this gambit with success in his so-called Atlanta Compromise. In it he implied that he and his people would for the time being accept an inferior social and political status in return for economic opportunity. "In all things that are purely social," he told a white audience (opposers), "we can be as separate as the fingers, yet one as the hand in all things essential to mutual progress."

Washington sincerely believed that through education the black man could achieve economic advancement and, possibly, sometime in the future, integration into American life. His "bargain" with the white people did accomplish a great deal in the education and training of black people. Whether it was worth the price is another matter. Within a year of the speech, in 1896, the Supreme Court endorsed the "separate but equal" doctrine for schools and soon afterwards the Southern states began to pass the Jim Crow laws that were to plague the South for many years.

Interorganizational. In another compromise, this time between the Democratic and Republican parties, the Democrats worked against their need for self-actualization.

The Presidential election of 1876 was close. Samuel J. Tilden, the Democratic candidate, was undoubtedly the winner, having a plurality of 250,000 votes, but there was a dispute over the electoral votes of three Southern states, where the returning boards dominated by Republicans certified electors that would vote for Rutherford B. Hayes. The confusion was compounded in Oregon, where one of the state's electoral votes was claimed by both the Democrats and the Republicans.

The Constitution has no provision for dealing with such a confused situation. Finally an Electoral Commission was set up, and with the tacit approval of Southern Democrats it had a pro-Hayes majority. The Democrats (negotiators) sacrificed their need for self-actualization—giving up the Presidency, for which they had a valid claim—but obtained a high price from the Republicans (opposers). The last federal troops, which had occupied the South after the Civil War, were withdrawn. Promptly the remaining Republican state governments in the South were voted out of office. The South also got one of its own into Hayes' cabinet and received generous amounts of federal funds for internal improvements. All in all it was not a bad bargain for the side that had lost the war only eleven years before.

International. At one point in the Cuban missile crisis in 1962, the United States (negotiator) worked against its need for self-actualization by giving up its initiative. The U.S. was using every type of pressure to get the missiles out of Cuba. Finally President Kennedy ordered a blockade of the island, and our ships of war stood directly in the path of all approaching Russian vessels. We told Russia (opposer) that if its ships continued on course and met our line of blockade, we would proceed to board and inspect them to see if they carried military cargoes. We thus gave up the initiative and left it to the Russians to determine what the next step in the negotiations would be. Fortunately for world peace, several Russian ships probably carrying contraband turned back. Russian ships with nonmilitary cargoes were allowed to proceed to Cuba unmolested.

5. NEGOTIATOR WORKS AGAINST THE OPPOSER'S SELF-ACTUALIZATION NEEDS

Interpersonal. Some companies (negotiators) have developed highly refined techniques for getting rid of an executive (opposer) without actually firing him. Their negotiations may run the gamut of his needs—from the safety need (cutting his pay) to the aesthetic need (removing the carpet from his office). But the company's task is difficult because it is trying to get the man to give up his more basic homeostatic need—the salary he requires to support himself and his family.

One of the most effective ways of getting an executive to quit is to work against his self-actualization need. For a man accustomed to making important decisions and being the center of attention, nothing is more devastating than to be deprived of his decision-making power and then be simply ignored. He will usually rationalize that taking a risk on his more basic needs by quitting and looking for a new job is a lesser evil than being deprived of his need for self-actualization.

Interorganizational. Sometimes top executives (negotiators) who fear losing their positions try to eliminate all acts of self-actualization in their subordinates (opposers). They perpetuate an authoritarian rule by doing away with all intercommunication. They recognize that, without information, the subordinates must depend upon them entirely for all decisions. Further, they cannot be criticized for honest judgment when they are the only ones with the facts.

International. When a nation attempts to pursue a self-actualization need, another country often cries "aggression." Although war in general, and wars of aggression in particular, are very much out of "fashion" these days, the nation that feels cheated will continue to fight the protector of a *status quo*. Pakistan's war with India over Kashmir is a typical example of an "aggressor," in this case Pakistan, trying to get what it considers its rightful territory. India, on the other hand, is willing to go to any lengths (except, apparently, negotiating the issue) to retain Kashmir; India (negotiators) thus works against Pakistan's (opposers) need for self-actualization.

6. NEGOTIATOR WORKS AGAINST THE OPPOSER'S AND HIS OWN SELF-ACTUALIZATION NEEDS

Interpersonal. When both parties to a dispute (negotiator and opposer) agree to place the matter in the hands of an arbitrator, then in a sense both sides are leaving the outcome to chance. By allowing an outsider to work out the solution, both sides have given up their need for self-actualization. One who feels strongly and capable of working to the fullness of his capacities will not usually turn the matter over to an independent arbitrator.

Interorganizational. The United States Constitution is an outstanding example of organizations, in this case states, giving up their self-actualization need. Under the Articles of Confederation the individual states were sovereign. This meant among other things that they could and did exact high tariffs for goods imported from neighboring states. This hampering of trade between the states was one of the main reasons for calling the Constitutional Convention. Fortunately the delegates went far beyond negotiations to ease trade restrictions and created a union of states in which each state (negotiator and opposer) gave up a degree of self-actualization for the more desirable goal of a strong central government.

International. The Washington Naval Agreement of 1922 was a well-intentioned but (for the United States) horrifying example of nations (negotiators and opposers) mutually working against their self-actualization needs. Great Britain had long depended on its navy to hold its far-flung empire together. The United States had tried to recapture the security that isolation from world affairs had once given it—meanwhile forgetting that twenty years before it had acquired a Pacific empire and was vitally concerned in Asian affairs. Yet both nations eagerly sought to limit the size of the navies of the major powers. In the agreement, the following ratios were decided on: Great Britain, 5; United States, 5; Japan, 3; France, 1.67; Italy, 1.67. Thus Japan, whose imperialist ambitions in Asia were becoming more and more apparent, was given a position of relative naval superiority in the Far East that it never could have obtained in a naval "arms race." In 1930 Japan's ratio was increased, but in 1935, when it was refused parity with Britain and the United States, it withdrew from the agreement. Despite this withdrawal and Japan's seizure of Manchuria, in the same year Britain, France, and the United States entered into a new agreement limiting the size of their navies!

VI. NEEDS TO KNOW AND UNDERSTAND

1. NEGOTIATOR WORKS FOR THE OPPOSER'S NEEDS TO KNOW AND UNDERSTAND

Interpersonal. Persuasion by using logic and reason is one of the most common and important negotiating techniques. Its most straightforward application, of course, is the clear, concise, accurate statement of facts. (In Chapters IV and V we discuss ways of determining facts in a situation.)

Interorganizational. Organizations also frequently negotiate by appealing to logic and fact. For example, if an independent group such as the Citizens' Union or the League of Women Voters endorses a political candidate, his party is certain to cite such independent endorsement during his campaign against opposing candidates. Nonpartisan support lends credibility to the party's (negotiator's) claims and arguments. Such support appeals to the voters' (opposers') need to know and to understand. Advertisers also use this gambit when they quote the endorsement of independent investigators such as the Consumer's Union, *Good Housekeeping* Magazine, or the American Dental Association. They seek through reason to persuade the consumer to buy their product, not their competitor's.

International. One of the most famous examples of working for an opposer's need to know and understand brought an end to the ten-year siege of Troy. The Greeks (the negotiators) pretended to abandon the siege but left behind a large wooden horse. The Trojans (the opposers) were "permitted" to learn that the horse was an offering to the gods. It had been made so large that it could not be brought through the gates of Troy. The Trojans, eager to make an offering to the goddess Athena, tore down part of their wall to bring the horse, and the Greek warriors it concealed, into the city.

2. NEGOTIATOR LETS THE OPPOSER WORK FOR HIS NEEDS TO KNOW AND UNDERSTAND

Interpersonal. When a girl (negotiator) tells her boyfriend (opposer), "I know, but I won't tell you," she is making him work for his needs to know and understand. The story of the unscrupulous optometrist (negotiator) and the way he sold a pair of glasses is an example of exploiting the customer's (opposer's) need to understand. Just when the customer thinks he understands, he is hit again by more bad news. The customer asks, "How much?" The optometrist replies, "Ten dollars." If there is no violent reaction from the customer, he then adds, "For the frames." Then he follows this with, "The lenses are five dollars." If the customer still remains silent, the tricky optometrist adds the word "each." In the negotiation the poor customer is striving to understand, to satisfy his need to know, and in this way falls a victim to this gambit.

Interorganizational. Using this gambit once got me out of a very bad business venture. Indeed, the situation might have proved financially disastrous. I had been persuaded to become involved in a hotel in Buffalo, New York, in a venture with one of my associates. Since I knew absolutely nothing about the hotel business, it was agreed in advance with my colleague that I should have no responsibility for the management of the property. Unfortunately, my associate suffered a crippling heart attack shortly after we signed the final papers. I was then obliged to take over the complete management of the hotel, which was losing $15,000 a month. Within three days I was to be called upon as the "expert" from New York City to tell the 500 employees in Buffalo how to do their jobs. I studied what the Harvard Business School had to offer on running hotels, but it was not much help. I sat at my desk and concentrated. Everything seemed against me. Then suddenly I had an idea. Nobody in Buffalo knew that I was hopelessly ignorant about running a hotel. A person would have to be crazy to become involved in a venture losing $15,000 a month if he didn't know anything about the business. Everyone (opposers) would assume that I (negotiator) was an expert on running hotels, so I decided that my gambit was to act the expert.

Arriving at the hotel, I told the manager to arrange appointments for me every fifteen minutes throughout the day. One by one, I interviewed every supervising employee as well as every person that sold the hotel food, supplies, or services. As each supervisor entered the room, I scowled and told him that I could no longer do business with him; I told each employee that he could no longer work for the hotel. Their jaws would drop, and then I would ask,

"How can I continue with anyone who is incompetent? You seem like a nice fellow, but I cannot tolerate the ridiculous things that have been going on." At this point they would try to justify their previous actions.

I would then say, "Only if you can tell me that you're at least aware of how things should be done, and if you can prove to me that you know what you're doing wrong—then perhaps we can still do business."

Each and every person I interviewed during the next few days poured forth a flood of suggestions, new approaches, and new methods for improving the management of the hotel. Without evaluating a single suggestion, I put the whole lot into operation. Within one month the loss was reduced to $1,000. The next month showed a profit of $3,000. By the time my associate left the hospital I was able to turn over to him a hotel that was firmly in the black. To put it simply, I let the other people work for their need to know and understand. They thought they knew I was an expert. I let them continue to think that they knew. And they never discovered my total ignorance of the hotel business.

International. In 1797 Secretary of State Timothy Pickering announced that 316 ships sailing under the American flag had been captured by the French the previous year. To avert war, President John Adams sent a commission of three men to negotiate a settlement with France. The American envoys reached Paris only to find that no one on the Directory, the five-man body then ruling France, would receive them. At last the Americans were approached by three mysterious Frenchmen, obviously the agents of Talleyrand, the French minister of foreign relations and one of the most powerful men in the world. The agents reported that before French-American negotiations could begin, the Directory must receive an apology from President Adams, a bribe of 1.2 million livres, and a "loan" of 32 million florins. These terms seemed not only excessive but insulting to the Americans, and they left France in a huff. Many Americans demanded a declaration of war against France when President Adams announced the tactics of the mysterious agents he named X, Y, and Z. In trying to make their opposer work for their need to know, arousing their curiosity, France (negotiator) had inadvertently worked against America's (opposer's) need for esteem—a disastrous maneuver in the case of the XYZ Affair.

3. Negotiator Works for the Opposer's and His Own Needs to Know and Understand

Interpersonal. Longfellow immortalized a famous negotiation based on the need for both negotiator and opposer to know and understand. When Miles Standish commissioned John Alden to present his proposal of marriage to Priscilla Mullens, Standish was working for his need to know Priscilla's interest. Priscilla (negotiator), however, had her own negotiation in mind. "Speak for yourself, John," said she, thereby working for her need to know and for that of John (her opposer) as well. Priscilla's gambit defined the area of discussion—always a good idea in a negotiation.

Interorganizational. Organizations also profit from defining the areas of disagreement early in a negotiation. Early agreement on issues speeds their settlement later on. One of the top men in the Conciliation Service in Washington used a method which, in his opinion, helped to effect a speedy settlement. After a hearing he was to mediate, he would restate the case to the parties, but he would deliberately mix up the terms and positions that each party represented to him. At this, both sides would be so appalled that they would go into a huddle and settle without more ado for fear that worse might befall them. Each party (negotiator and opposer) in this instance was working for the need to know and to understand itself and the other. I feel, however, that the mediator caused both parties to lose faith in mediation as a means of reaching a settlement; and thus he performed a disservice to his function.

The following is a more positive way of working for a mutual need to know and understand.

Trade associations are faced with many problems, particularly in connection with the antitrust laws and price fixing. Price fixing by an association is illegal. There are, however, many things that trade associations can do legally in this field. For example, associations have initiated programs to educate their members in cost accounting procedures. The members are shown how to calculate the actual costs in their industry. They are then shown how to apply this data to their individual business by using uniform methods of accounting. After being thoroughly indoctrinated in this way, it is unlikely that any member will sell at prices below those that the association accountants suggest as the minimum. This is a form of negotiation in which each member works for his own and his competitor's (opponent's) joint need to know and understand.

International. One of the most successful gambits used by the United States (negotiator) to work for both its own and its opposer's need to know and understand is the Fulbright Act passed in 1946. By financing student exchanges, the United States promoted understanding of far greater scope than the specific study programs of the scholars. Foreign hosts learned to know and understand Americans. Americans learned to know and to understand other countries. More than twenty-five nations participated in the program, including America's enemies in World War II, Japan, Italy, and Germany, although unfortunately East Germany, as well as other Iron Curtain countries, did not take part. In this case, the more basic needs prevented meaningful negotiations between nations.

4. NEGOTIATOR WORKS AGAINST HIS NEEDS TO KNOW AND UNDERSTAND

Interpersonal. We all have the need to know and understand, but sometimes in order to negotiate successfully, it is essential that we work against that need. For example, when a husband (the opposer) is unfaithful to his wife, the signs of his disaffection can be quite obvious. Rather than ask questions and provoke an unpleasant negotiation, his wife (the negotiator) may decide to remain quiet, to pretend to misunderstand what she sees. She gives up her need to know, tries to improve her marriage in more subtle ways, and leads her opposition toward a face-saving solution for them both.

Interorganizational. Sometimes in the course of a negotiation we may decide to stake the outcome on faith or to rely on luck. A religious organization might resort to such a negotiating gambit. And one of the most obvious examples in which a religious group consistently sacrifices the need to know, in the scientific sense, is when the Jehovah's Witnesses (negotiators) refuse a blood transfusion, even when advised by physicians (opposers) that it may be a matter of life or death.

International. The U.S. ban on American reporters visiting Red China works against America's (negotiator's) need to know and understand its opposer. Working against the need to know is not always to a nation's disadvantage, however. During the Cuban crisis between the United States and Russia in 1962, the following negotiation took place between President Kennedy and Chairman Khrushchev. President Kennedy had, for some unexplained reason, received two conflicting messages from Khrushchev. One message contained terms that were acceptable; the other did not. What should be done? In an August 4, 1964, article in the New York *World Telegram and Sun,* Roger Hilsman wrote: "It was Robert Kennedy who conceived a brilliant diplomatic maneuver. Later dubbed the 'Trollope ploy,' after the recurrent theme in Anthony Trollope's novels in which the girl interprets a squeeze of her hand as a proposal of marriage, Robert Kennedy's suggestion was to deal with . . . the acceptable message only, and to ignore the other message." Kennedy said that he would accept Khrushchev's offer and then went on to set forth his own ideas of what that offer was.

Khrushchev knew that he had sent two contradictory messages, but the President's (opposer's) gambit allowed Khrushchev (the negotiator) to give up his need to know and understand, and to accept the Kennedy interpretation of the two messages.

5. Negotiator Works Against the Opposer's Needs to Know and Understand

Interpersonal. People (negotiators) often work against their opposer's need to know by omitting important facts in order to give a misleading impression. Mothers are wont to use this negotiating gambit with their children. How many times has "Drink your milk, dear" concealed the fact that Johnnie will drink his milk *plus* his medicine?

It is also possible to try to gain the advantage in a negotiation by creating misunderstandings and exploiting your opposer's need to know. The following example illustrates this gambit.

A Mr. J. Robert LeShufy (opposer) asked me to represent him in a purchase of land on Staten Island at the time of feverish activity preceding the building of the Verrazano Bridge from Brooklyn. The seller (negotiator) with whom I was to negotiate was one of the largest landowners. I soon learned that he had a reputation as a shrewd bargainer, that he never closed a deal until he was convinced that he had obtained the best possible price. I also learned that he used a technique that I call "plateau" negotiation. An agent of this shrewd seller would meet with you, bargain about the price, and then shake hands on what you believed to be the agreed price and terms of the sale. But when you met the actual seller, you would find out that the terms were only those on which *you* had agreed to buy, but not those on which he had agreed to *sell*. He had worked on your need to know and understand and had subtly misled you. The seller himself then took up some item that had not been discussed previously and would use it as a wedge to get a raise in price or more favorable terms. He tried to raise you to a new plateau, to face you with the alternative of agreeing to the new terms or calling off the deal. He might use the strategy of demanding that title be taken within fifteen days instead of the customary forty-five to sixty days after the contract is signed. He would use this new demand to extract fresh concessions from the buyer. He had employed these devices so often that he could gauge the point where the buyer would rather withdraw than meet the new demand. With the "plateau" technique, it is not rare for the seller to take up his pen, ready to sign the final drafted contract, only to put it down again and continue to negotiate on one last condition. The great skill was in knowing when the opposer's patience had been stretched to its limit.

LeShufy could recognize this technique as soon as it was tried on him. He had come up with a counter-move, which I call "exposure." After the first attempt to push him to a new plateau, LeShufy smiled and began to tell a story. It concerned a fictional character whom he called Mr. Dorf. LeShufy said that he could never buy land from Mr. Dorf because every time he thought he had a deal worked out, Mr. Dorf would keep pushing and pushing him. Dorf was never satisfied until the terms of the deal were past their absolute limits. "Exposure" proved to be a powerful counter-move. Every time the seller tried to "plateau," LeShufy would look directly at the seller, smile, and say, "Now, now, you are acting just like Mr. Dorf." It never failed to halt the seller dead in his tracks and put a stop to his "plateau" maneuver. "Exposure" was a powerful countermove because it was based on the esteem need, which is more basic than the need to know and understand. This is in agreement with the principle that *the more effective gambit is the one that employs the more basic need.*

Interorganizational. You (negotiator) can occasionally work against your opposer's need to know and understand by giving out entirely too much information. You do this intentionally to confuse the opposition and make it difficult for him to follow the details of the negotiation. By presenting an overabundance of information, you manage to hide many of the vital facts. In government, budgets are often passed by using this negotiating gambit. It is also found useful in preventing stockholders from understanding too much when they read a corporation's annual report.

International. This gambit is used in intelligence and counter-intelligence work. It involves all the spy techniques from propaganda to elaborate deceptions—such as the Allies (the negotiators) used to make Germany (the opposer) think the invasion of Europe would come at Calais instead of Normandy. Whenever misinformation is intentionally given out—and used—it works against an opposer's need to know and understand.

6. NEGOTIATOR WORKS AGAINST THE OPPOSER'S AND HIS OWN NEEDS TO KNOW AND UNDERSTAND

Interpersonal. If you (negotiator) and your opposer agree to leave the outcome of a negotiation to chance by abiding by a flip of a coin, or a roll of the dice, then you are working against your need to know and understand, and your opposer is working against his same need. You both have decided to leave the decision to the independent determination of an outside event.

Interorganizational. Rivalry can easily lead to silence, secrecy, and suspicion on the part of all parties. Certainly intraservice rivalry among the U.S. Army, Navy, and Air Force following World War II had this result. The trend toward a more centralized defense program threatened many servicemen whose loyalty to their own branch of the service outweighed other considerations. On too many occasions, the need for service esteem superseded not only the need to know but the needs of national security as well. Yet, whatever one may think of the results, all three services (negotiators) used this gambit in dealing with Congress (the opposer) regarding appropriations and with Congressional efforts to have a deciding voice in the Defense Department. Each wanted Congress to give greater weight to its individual request—regardless of its relative importance and the facts presented.

International. The San Juan boundary dispute between the United States and Great Britain in the nineteenth century is a clear case of each party working against its need to know. The

1844 Democratic National Convention slogan "Fifty-four forty or fight" resulted in the Compromise Treaty of 1846. The Oregon Treaty of 1846 described the boundary between the British and American territory on the Northwest Pacific Coast as "the channel that separates the continent from Vancouver Island." In point of fact, the coastline was marked by several channels dividing the various San Juan Islands from each other and from the mainland. The British naturally claimed that the channel referred to was the Rosario Strait, which would make most of the islands British. The United States claimed that it was the Haro Strait, which would make all the islands American.

Each nation tried to prove its point by force. In 1853 the Hudson's Bay Company started to farm sheep on one of the islands. The United States claimed the farm owed the U.S. taxes. When the Company refused to pay, the U.S. tax collector confiscated some sheep. Ensuing incidents became really serious when a pig belonging to the Company's agent, Charles Griffin, crawled under a fence and ate some potatoes belonging to an American settler, Lyman Cutler. Infuriated, Cutler shot the pig on its second foray. Griffin threatened to arrest Cutler and send him to England for trial. In response to a request for military protection, the United States sent in Captain George Pickett with sixty soldiers to guard American settlers. The governor of Vancouver retaliated by sending three warships to the area. Fortunately neither side fired a shot, and a joint patrol of the area was set up.

During the American Civil War, the "Pig War" quieted down to some degree, but still neither side could negotiate a solution. Finally, in 1871, both nations gave up their need to know and and turned to an independent arbitrator, William I of Germany. He applied some reason and logic to the thorny problem, measured the various channels, and decided that the deepest was the correct boundary line. Because this was Haro Strait, the San Juan islands belonged to the United States.

VII. AESTHETIC NEEDS

1. NEGOTIATOR WORKS FOR THE OPPOSER'S AESTHETIC NEEDS

Interpersonal. To start a negotiation by making an excessive demand and then suddenly offering to split the difference is an all too frequent method of negotiating. When you (negotiator) do this, you are working on your opposer's need for balance and symmetry. However, it may be a dangerous tactic, because if the original demand is too unrealistic, it will discourage further bargaining and even bring matters to a dead stop. I have seen many insurance adjusters refuse to discuss a settlement when the opposing attorney has led off with a demand beyond all reason.

In line with this gambit one's position may become more balanced and acceptable if it is related to an unconnected external fact, precedent, pattern, or principle.

Interorganizational. In the world of fashion, the designer (negotiator) works for the need of the prospective buyer (opposer); he plays upon the buyer's aesthetic need. The designer sets the fashions, displays the styles, and the buyer may simply look and thereby be persuaded. He climbs on the bandwagon so that he will be sure to buy goods that are "in style."

International. In negotiations between nations that do not share a common set of values, it is often advantageous to agree upon the formal rules that will govern the conference and the agenda for the meeting. With the negotiator working for the opposing nation's aesthetic need for form and order, the meeting may be directed into constructive channels. In many negotiations with the Free World, Russia has used this gambit with such regularity that deciding on the rules and the agenda often consumes more time and effort than the negotiations themselves.

2. NEGOTIATOR LETS THE OPPOSER WORK FOR HIS AESTHETIC NEEDS

Interpersonal. When a sales clerk (negotiator) faces the customer (opposer) across the counter of a retail store, he often uses this gambit. Large retail organizations have trained their sales personnel to make the customer work for his aesthetic need. They try to lead the customer to the most balanced path, the line of least resistance, the most symmetrical view. Often a customer will buy when he sees other people buying. He is more apt to order a "large" orange drink if he is asked, "Do you want a large drink?" than if he is asked, "Do you want a large or small drink?"

Interorganizational. When a company provides an orderly atmosphere, with everything arranged and organized, it is offering the opposition an opportunity to work for its aesthetic need. This

is also true when the negotiator presents his opposer an almost
completed job and allows him to finish it. Sales promotions that
get the consumer interested in a product by offering prizes for
completing jingles or finishing crossword puzzles are examples
of this gambit.

International. Antonio López de Santa Anna, Mexican general
and dictator, used this gambit very effectively during the Mexican-
American War. President James K. Polk was determined to have
California and all other Mexican lands between Texas and the
Pacific Ocean. He hoped to get the land by purchase, but when
this failed he resorted to war. Within a year American troops occupied all the land that Polk desired. However, he could not persuade the Mexican government to acknowledge the fact in a peace
treaty.

Santa Anna (negotiator), who had been deposed in 1844,
played on Polk's (opposer's) aesthetic need for recognition of a
de facto situation to get what he wanted: return to power. He
offered Polk a peace treaty if the United States would engineer
his return to Mexico. In August 1846 Santa Anna was passed
through the U.S. naval blockade and landed at Veracruz. He ral-
lied his supporters and quickly seized the government. However,
in a typical example of honor among thieves, he announced that
he would not accept a peace treaty and would recover Mexico's
lost territory. It took the United States a year of hard fighting to de-
pose Santa Anna and force a peace settlement on the new Mexican government.

3. Negotiator Works for the Opposer's and His Own Aesthetic Needs

Interpersonal. A negotiator makes an appeal to the need for
orderliness, the aesthetic need, by reading the terms under negotiation over and over again and, temporarily ignoring the items
not agreed to, listing all the points that *are* settled. This work of
bringing order out of chaos feeds the opposer's sense of aesthetics
and often facilitates a solution.

Interorganizational. Sometimes, in negotiations, questions such
as who should be the chairman, or what items should be placed
on the agenda, assume great importance and cause endless bicker-
ing. This problem has been successfully solved by the negotiating
device of a rotating chairman as well as a rotating agenda. Such

an approach works for the aesthetic needs of all parties. Each day one of the parties to the negotiation has its representative in the chair and its most important item heads the agenda. The next day it changes. This idea of rotation may also be applied to reports on negotiation progress, each party's report heading the list in turn.

International. The cultural exchange program conducted by Russia (opposer) and the United States (negotiator) is an example of this gambit on the international level. The high value that each nation attaches to the program is indicated by the attention each gives to ensuring that it sends as many artists as the other does.

4. NEGOTIATOR WORKS AGAINST HIS AESTHETIC NEEDS

Interpersonal. Many times you (negotiator) are forced to accept the gambit of working against your aesthetic need. People creating an artistic work, or writing a book, or decorating their house, often become impatient and sacrifice their aesthetic need just to get the work finished. This also can be used when dealing with someone else. Therefore, when you (negotiator), after a long ordeal, say to the other side (opposer), "Let's get the thing over with," you may add new impetus to the negotiations.

Many religious customs and traditions, when viewed historically, can be considered negotiating gambits. In the late Middle Ages, among the Eastern European Jews, a married woman was required to shave off all the hair on her head. The Jewish woman (negotiator) gave up this aesthetic need as protection (negotiation) against violation by mobs (opposers) in times of anti-Jewish excesses. Feminine vanity, however, brought about the introduction of the use of the "sheitel," or wig, which was sometimes made from the hair clipped from the wearer's own head. These wigs were worn, however, at times when no danger threatened the Ghetto.

Interorganizational. The City of New York applied a new method of real estate assessment in its taxation of the Seagram Building on Park Avenue. The city refused to give the building's owners any allowance for the beautiful construction of the ground floor park, pool, and arcade. Indeed, the tax was raised about 200 per cent. A *New York Times* article called the new ap-

proach a "tax on beauty." In this instance New York City (negotiator) was working against its need for aesthetics in order to
achieve a greater income. This negotiation might be short-sighted
and cause the city to suffer because builders (opposers) will be
even more inclined to put up the most prosaic low-tax structures.
    International. When the United States (negotiator) sends dis-
plays of its latest new schools of art abroad, thus courting ridicule,
it is, in a sense, giving up its aesthetic need. However, what this
does do is show the world (opposer) the freedom that exists in the
United States. As a negotiating gambit this carries a larger message.

5. NEGOTIATOR WORKS AGAINST THE OPPOSER'S AESTHETIC NEEDS

    Interpersonal. You (negotiator) can work against your opposer's
need for aesthetics by arguing the merits of conformity to tradi-
tion. When you are confronted with an advanced type of aesthetic thinking, you may condemn it merely because it does not conform. This same tactic can be used to downgrade new ideas, new
art, new styles, and new concepts. Many people will attempt to
prove their position, not on facts or reason, but merely on the
basis of conformity to the present acceptable taste—today's mother
insisting on her son's getting a specific type of haircut.
    Interorganizational. Whenever a beautiful building, an historic
landmark, or some decorative relic of the past is torn down to
make way for a luxury apartment or an office building, we may say
that the builders (negotiators) are working against the public's
(opposer's) aesthetic need. The old and the beautiful are economically unsound because the new structures "pay better." This
argument is advanced *ad nauseum* in the welter of new building
programs that are destroying many lovely structures on Manhat-
tan Island and elsewhere, replacing them with *only* tax-paying and
economically utilized constructions.
    International. Japan (negotiator) used this gambit in the nine-
teenth century when the United States (opposer) was attempting
to open the country to Western trade. The Japanese tried to avoid
dealing with the Western world and referred to them as aesthetic
"barbarians." Their motive was to conceal the essential weakness
of the nation. Only a display of gunboat diplomacy brought an
end to this very effective gambit.

6. Negotiator Works Against the Opposer's and His Own Aesthetic Needs

Interpersonal. You (negotiator) can work against the aesthetic needs of both yourself and your opposer by the gambit of injecting humor into the negotiation. To laugh and joke is to distract, and is most helpful when a situation becomes tense. Humor has been defined as the playful, ridiculous, unbalanced attitude, and as such it might be considered as working against our need for balance and order.

Interorganizational. The huge billboards that so frequently mar the scenic beauty of our highways furnish an example of all parties working against their aesthetic needs. The state (opposer) allows the signs because they collect taxes on them, and the sign company (negotiator) puts them up for profits. Recognizing the economic reasons for this defacement of natural beauty, the federal government has offered money incentives to states that prohibit billboards on major highways.

International. Thomas Jefferson's introduction of "pell mell" to the White House had international repercussions and is a wild example of this gambit. Although Jefferson (negotiator) was a Virginia aristocrat and a gracious host, he decided when he became President that his manners should reflect republican simplicity and informality. Therefore, when he received the British minister (opposer) and his wife, he was dressed in a worn-out suit and bedroom slippers. The couple, resplendently attired, was naturally shocked, but much worse was to come. Jefferson announced at White House dinners that "pell mell and next-the-door form the basis of etiquette in the societies of this country."

At the first dinner they attended, the British minister and his wife were almost trampled to death when dinner was announced. In the dining room they had to scramble for seats at the table. Their only consolation was that Jefferson had a superb French chef. The minister, consulting with other foreign diplomats, decided this was an insult to all their countries. But in spite of protests, pell mell remained the White House custom throughout Jefferson's Presidency.

Although the custom sacrificed every aesthetic principle of polite society, Jefferson was willing to give up his and the minister's aesthetic needs to win over the American voters. He was not the first nor the last American politician to curry favor with the voters by twisting the British lion's tail..

XI

SUCCESS

In conclusion, our study of the art of negotiation has included an examination of the philosophy and psychology of negotiating, and the preparation that is necessary beforehand. We have considered human behavior, both in its relation to negotiation and its connection with fundamental human needs. We have evolved the Need Theory of Negotiation, the variety of application to various types of needs, the methods for recognizing needs, and finally the proper planning of strategy.

Negotiation is a tool of human behavior, a tool anyone can use effectively. I have tried to avoid shaping it into a specialized tool that would be suitable for use only by professionals. I have sought to give the realm of negotiation new forms that are allied to the forms of other types of human activities.

The successful negotiator must combine the alertness and speed of an expert swordsman with an artist's sensitivity. He must watch his adversary across the bargaining table with the keen eye of a fencer, ever ready to spot any loophole in the defense, any shift in strategy. He is prepared to thrust at the slightest opportunity. On the other hand, he must also be the sensitive artist, perceptive of the slightest variation in the color of his opponent's mood or motivation. At the correct moment he must be able to select from his palette of many colors exactly the right combination of shades and tints that will lead to mastery. Success in negotiation, aside from adequate training, is essentially a matter of sensitivity and correct timing.

Finally, the mature negotiator will have an understanding of the cooperative pattern. He will try to achieve agreement and will remember that in a successful negotiation everyone wins.

And if this is the case, why shoot it out, when we can still talk it out?

INDEX